This Book Belongs To :

....

....

COLOR TEST

TEST YOUR COLOR SUPPLIES ON THIS PAGE

TO SEE HOW THEY REACT TO THE PAPER.

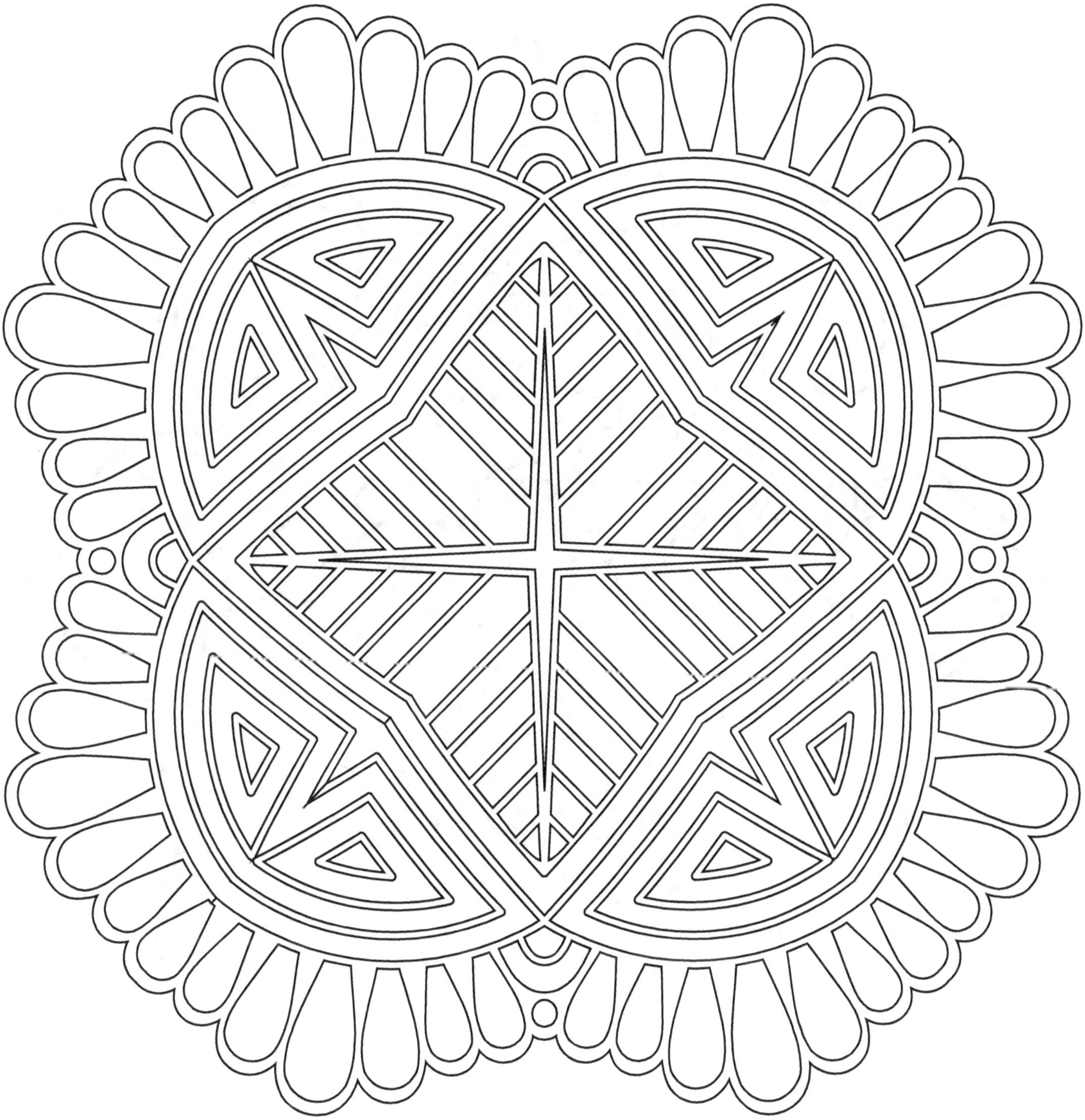

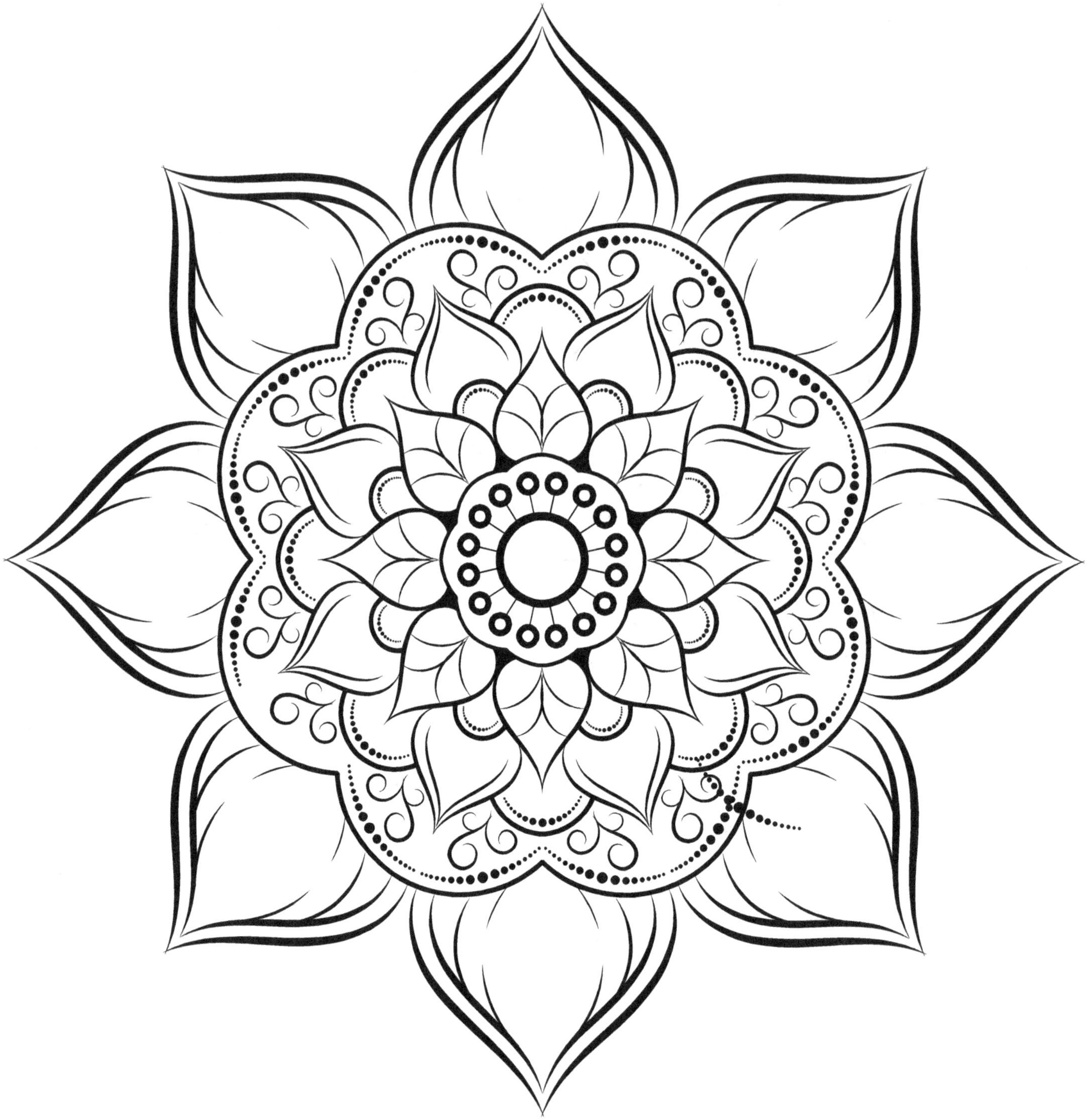

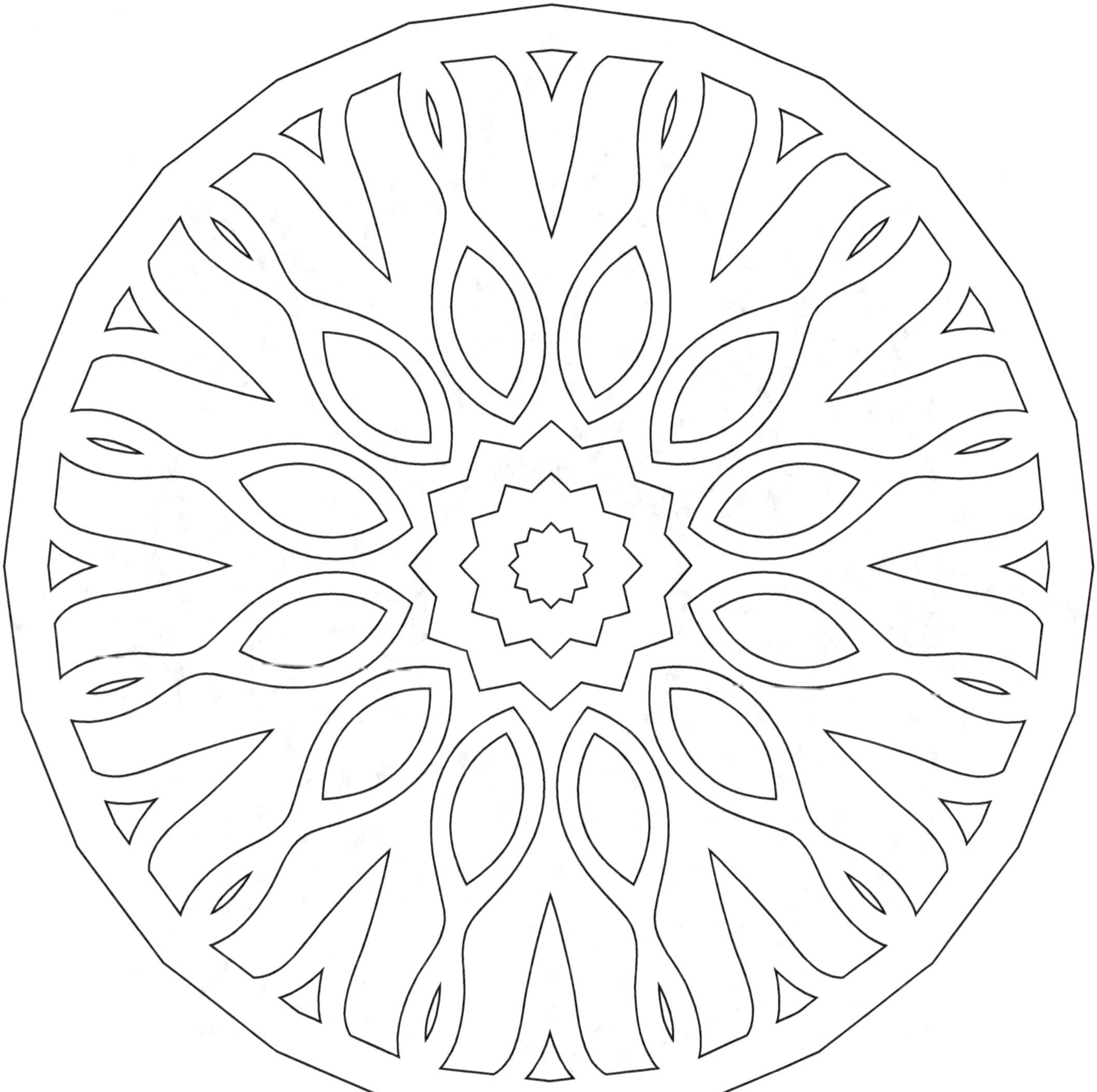

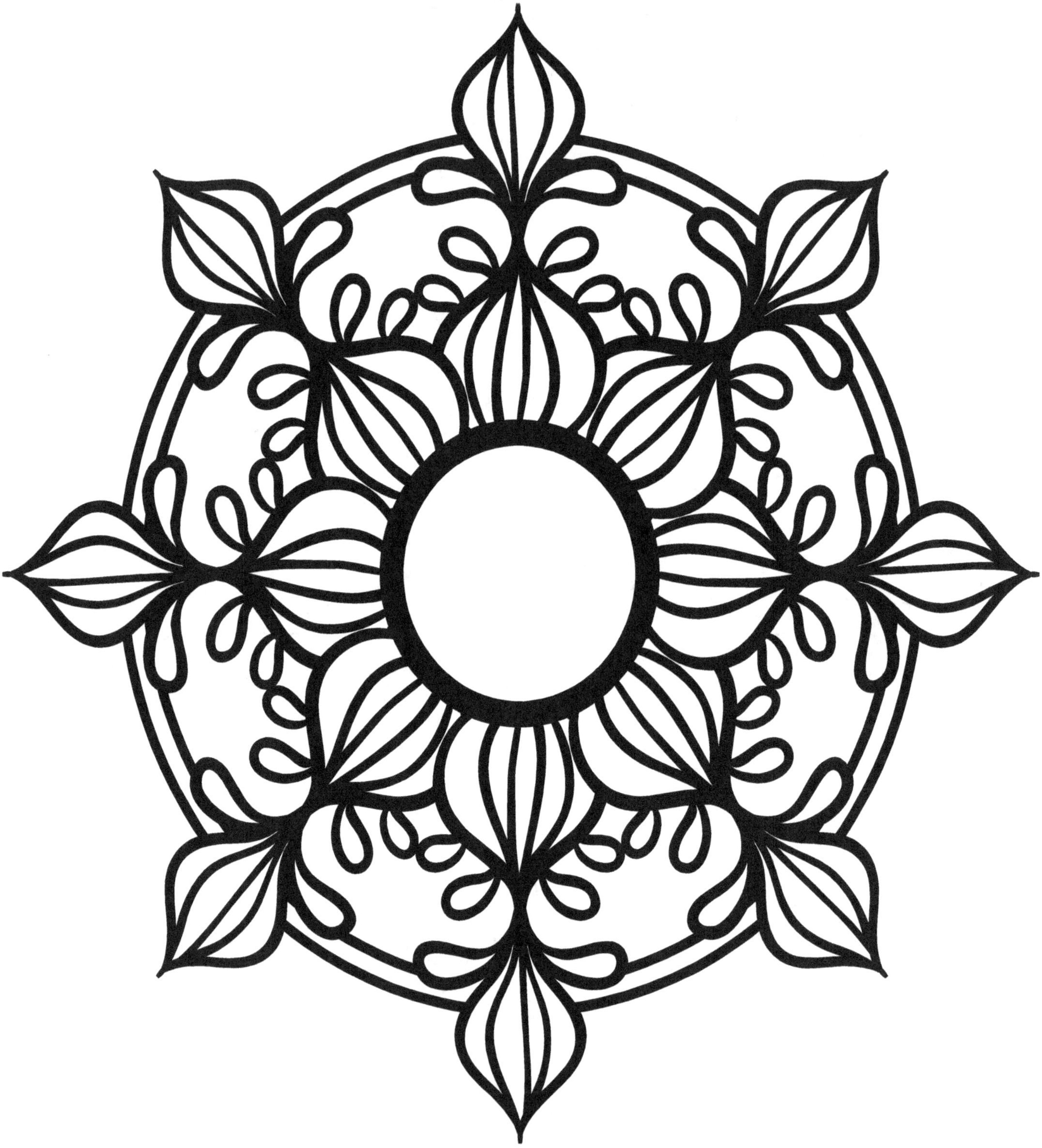

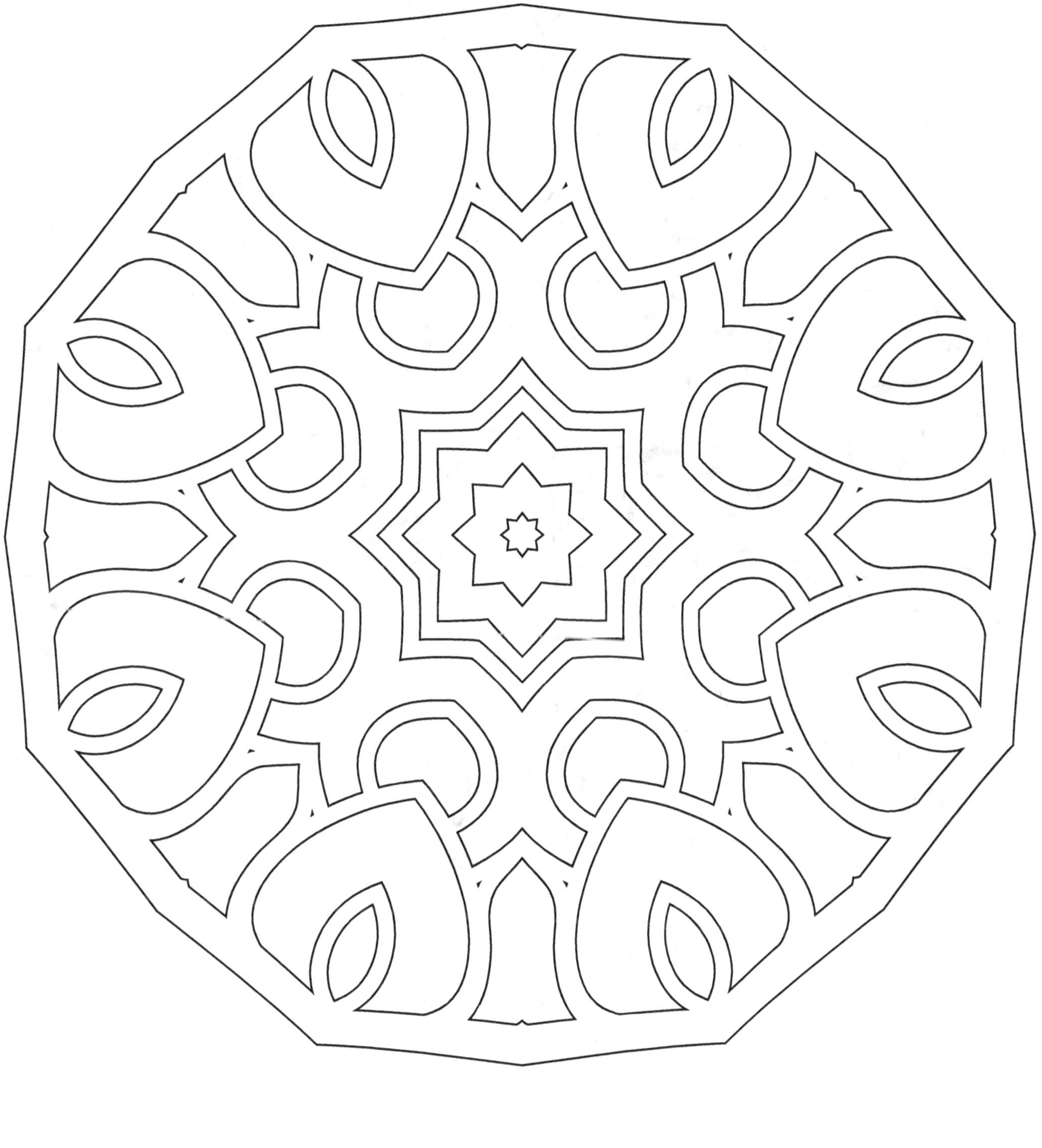

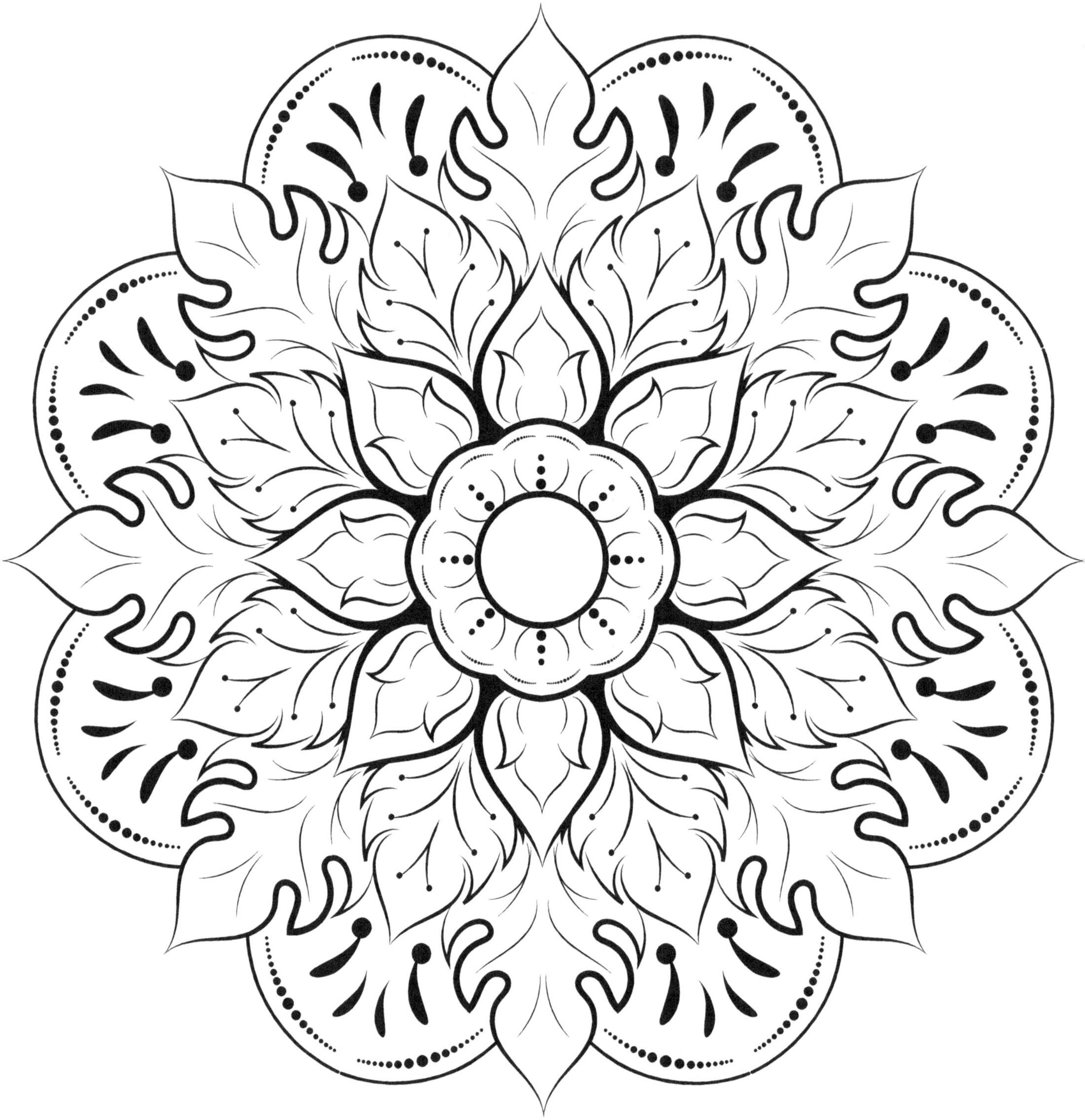

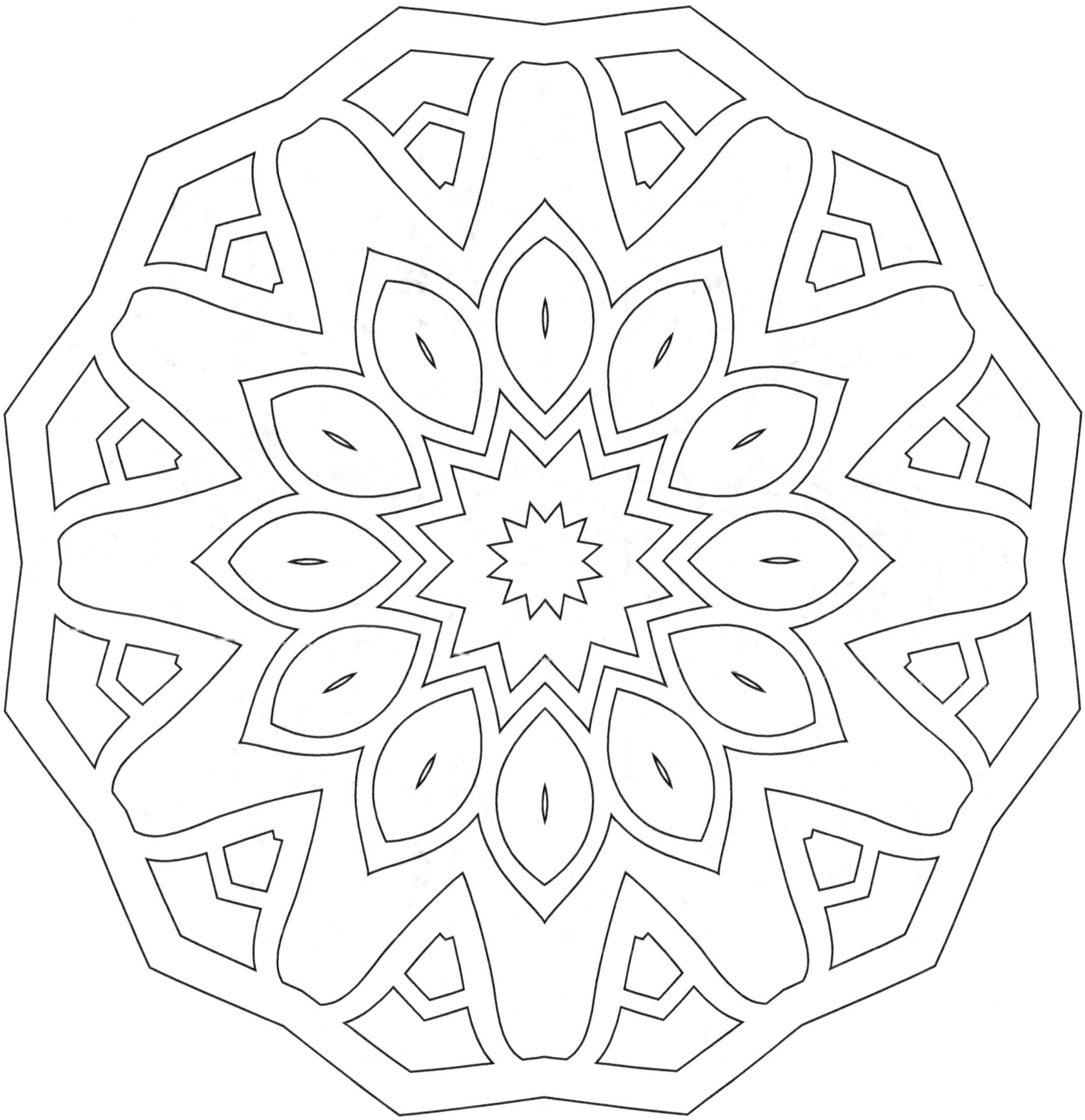

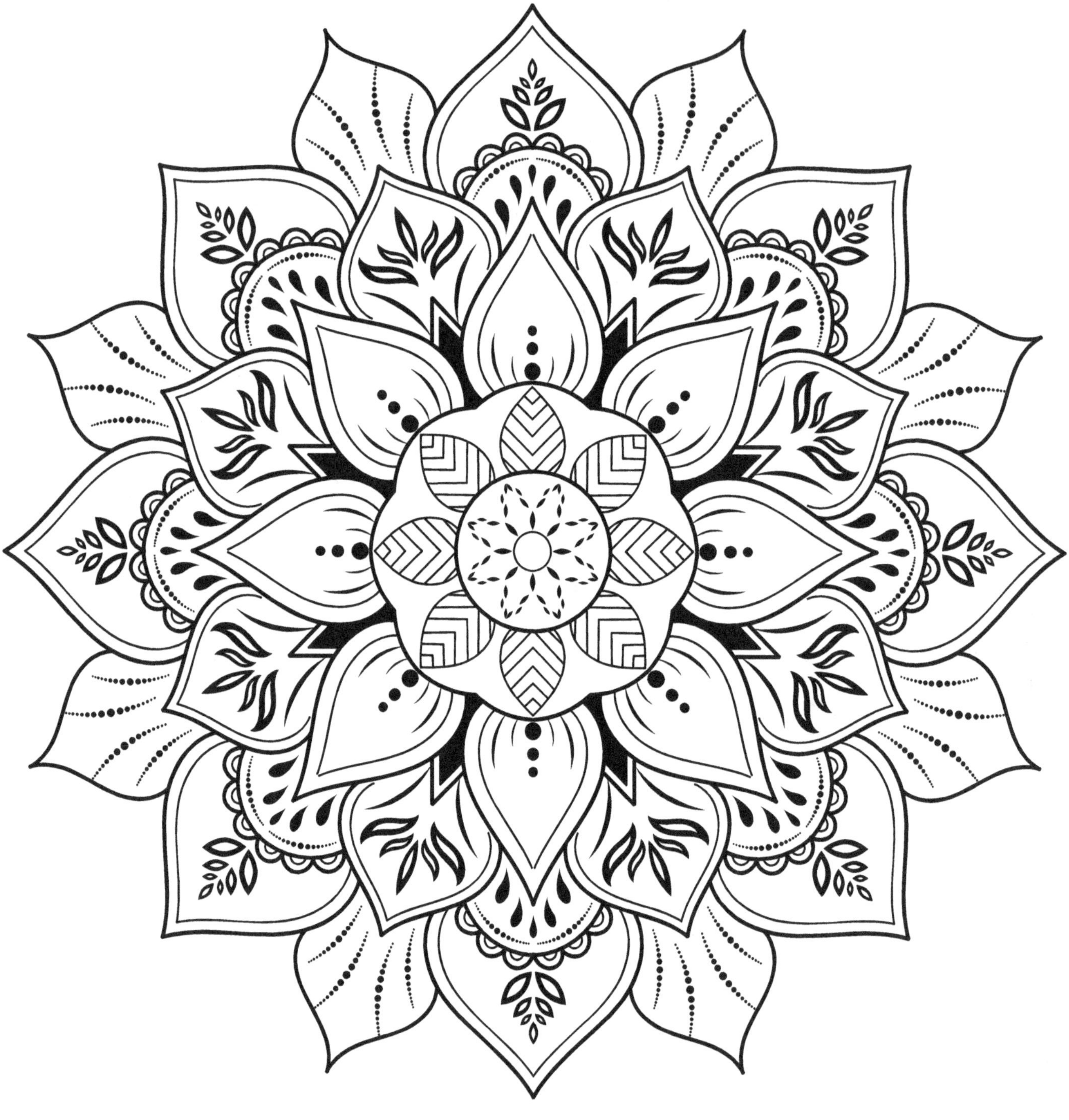

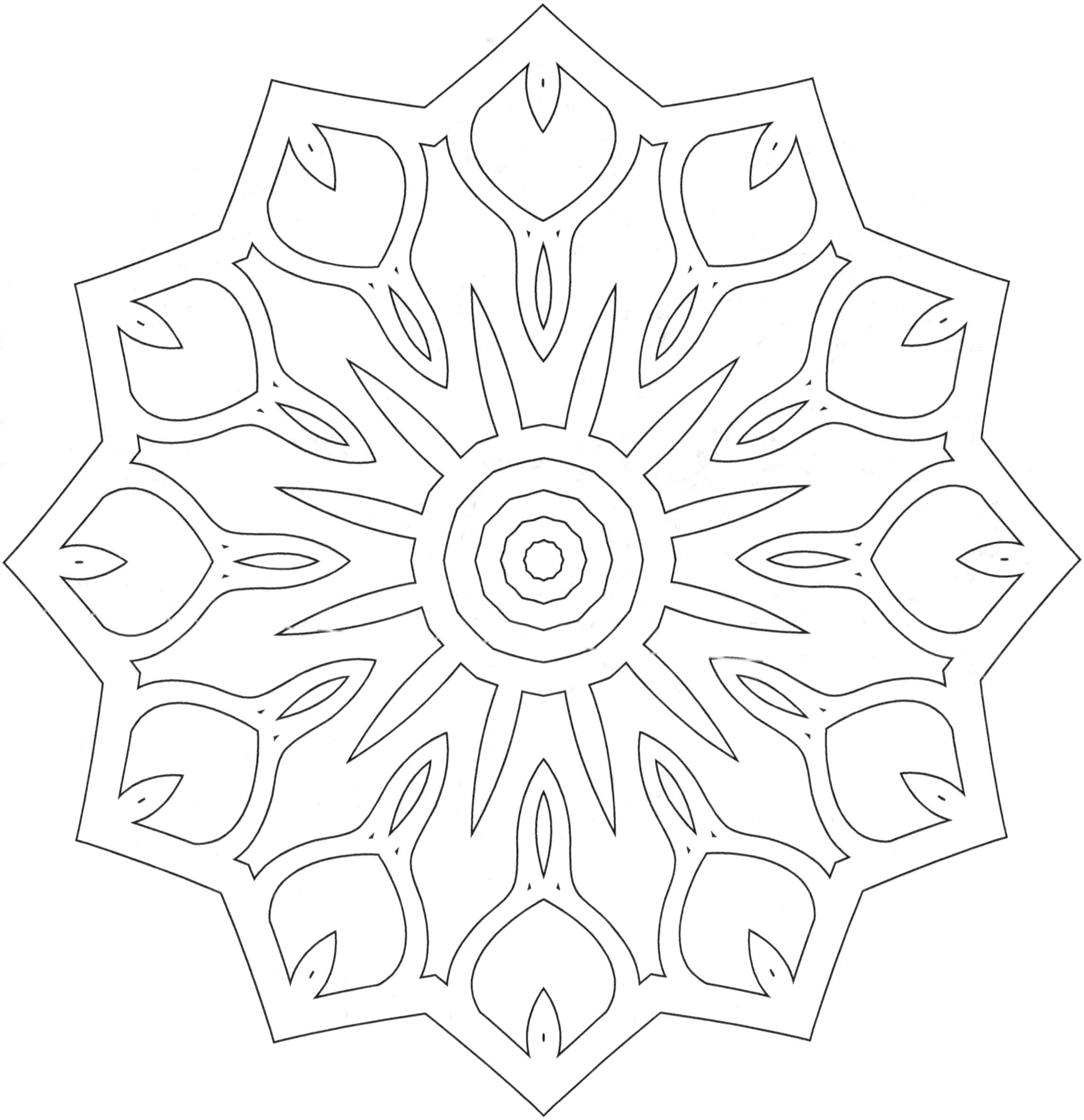

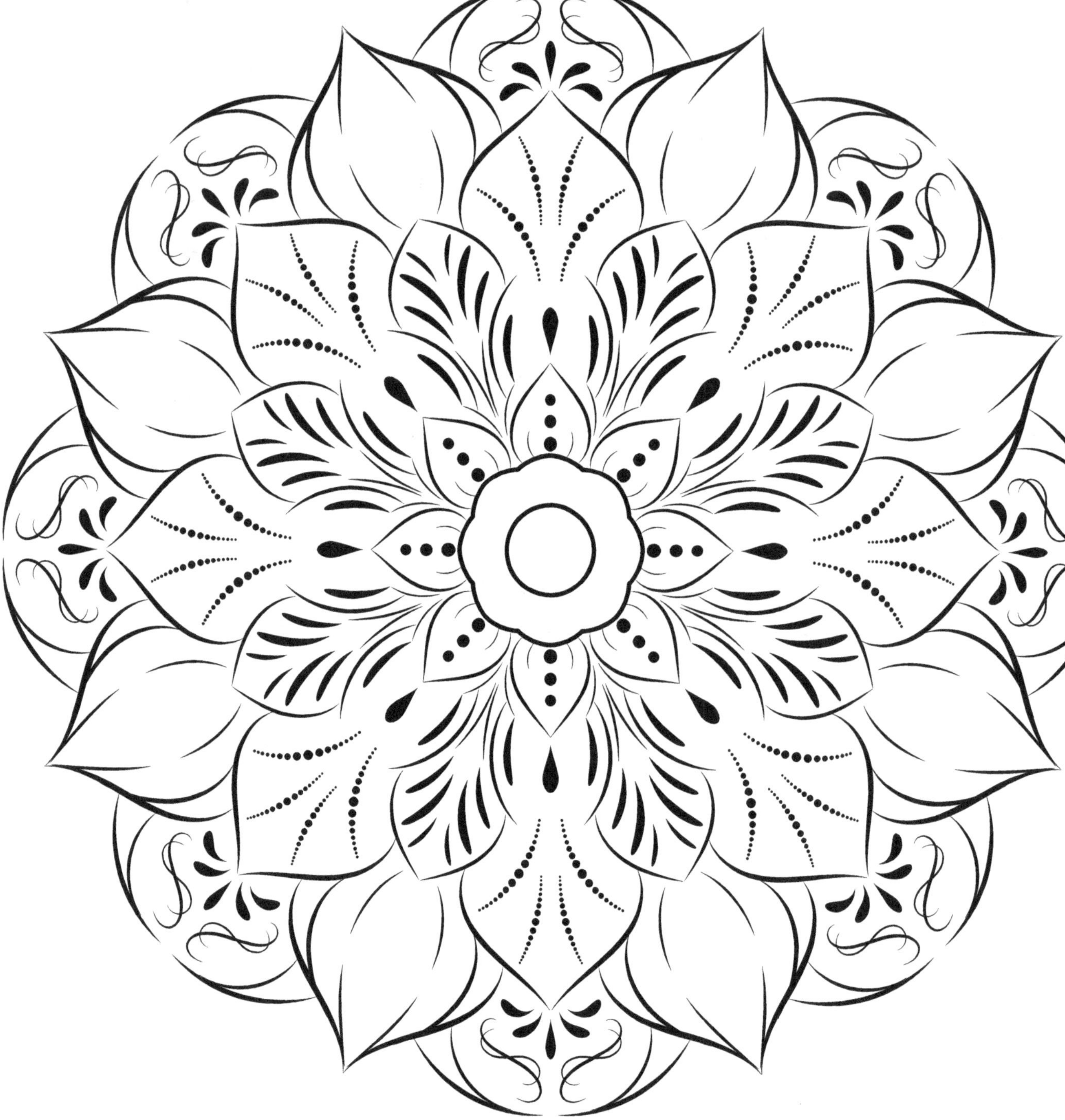

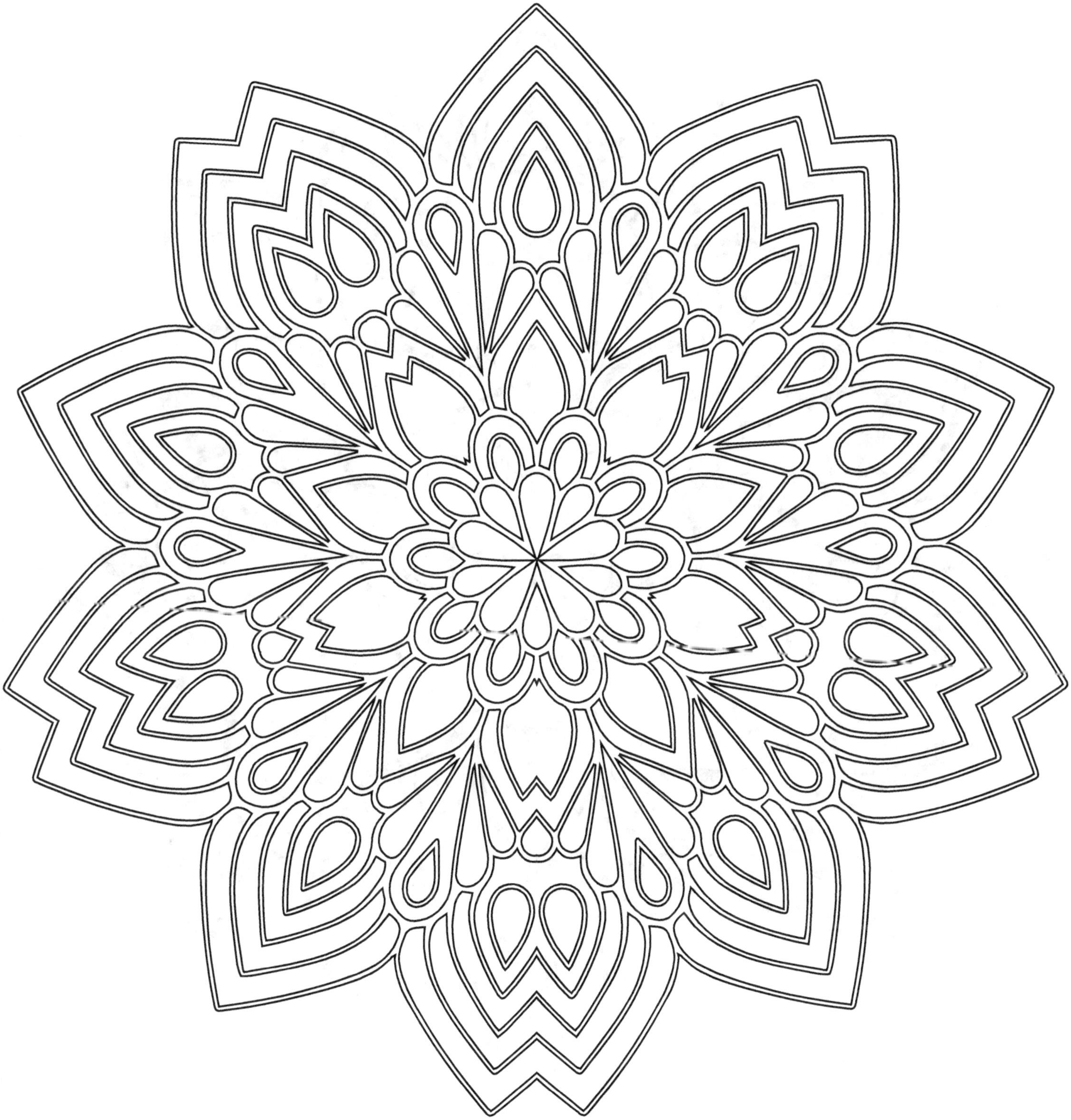

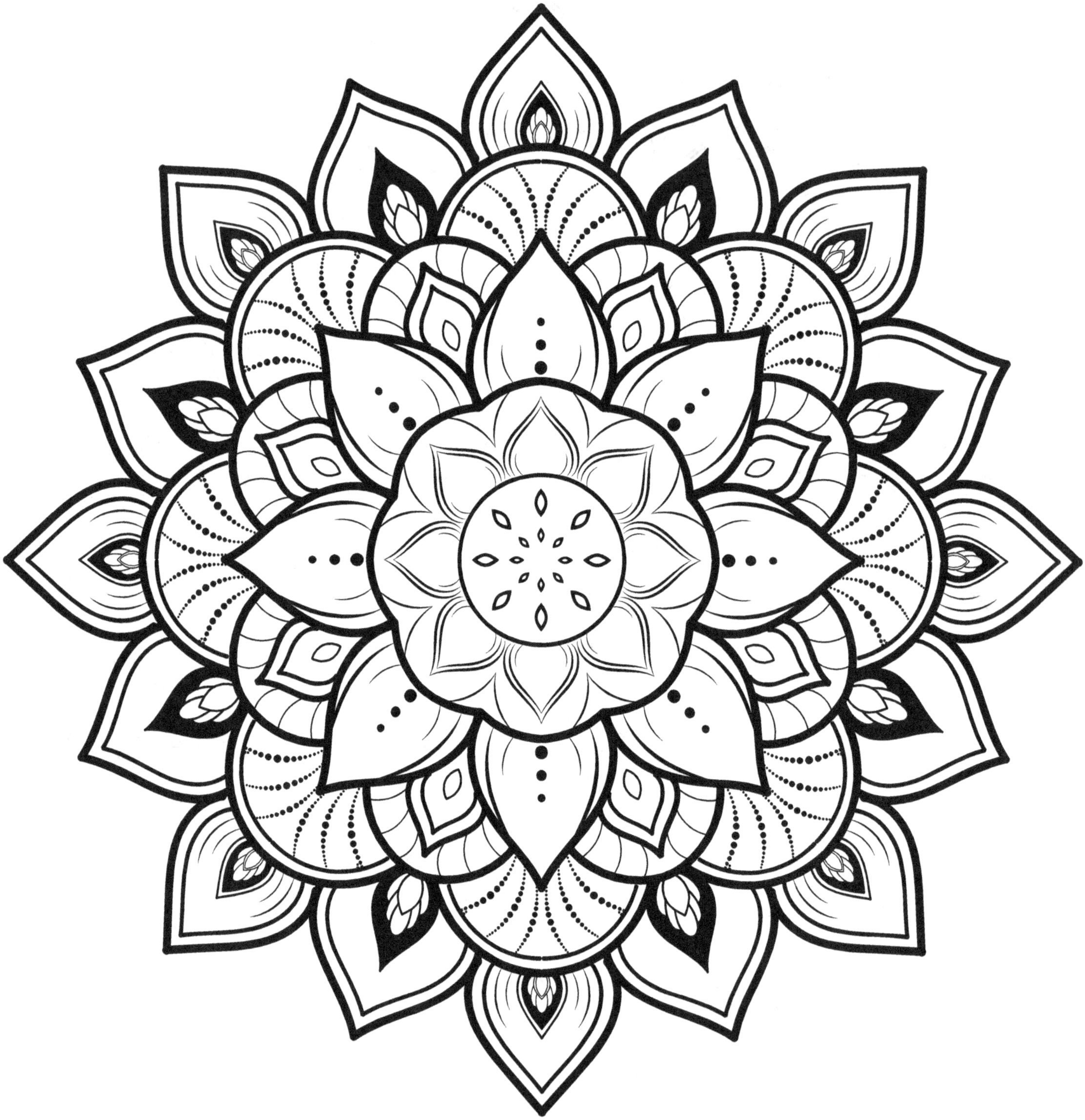

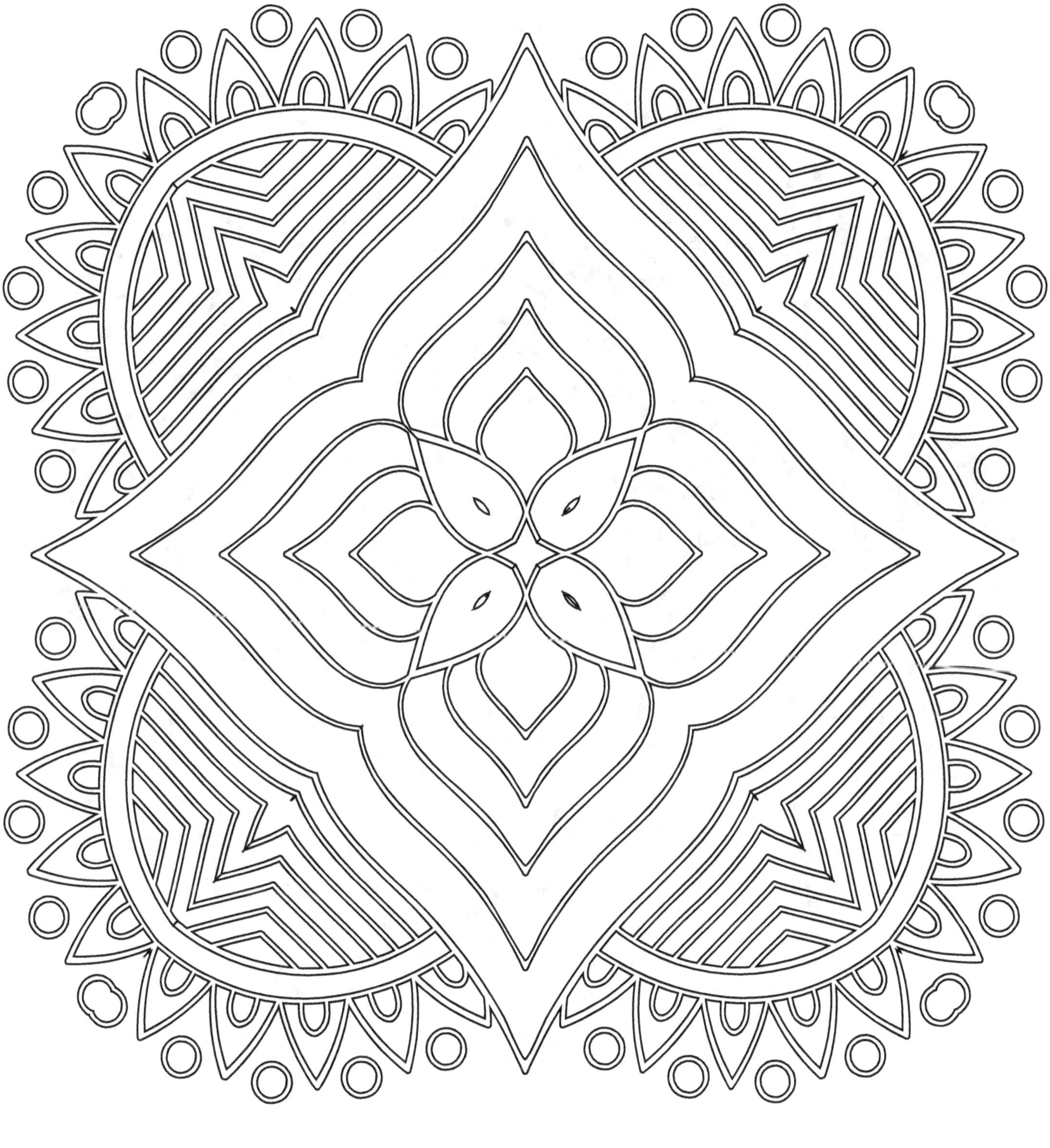

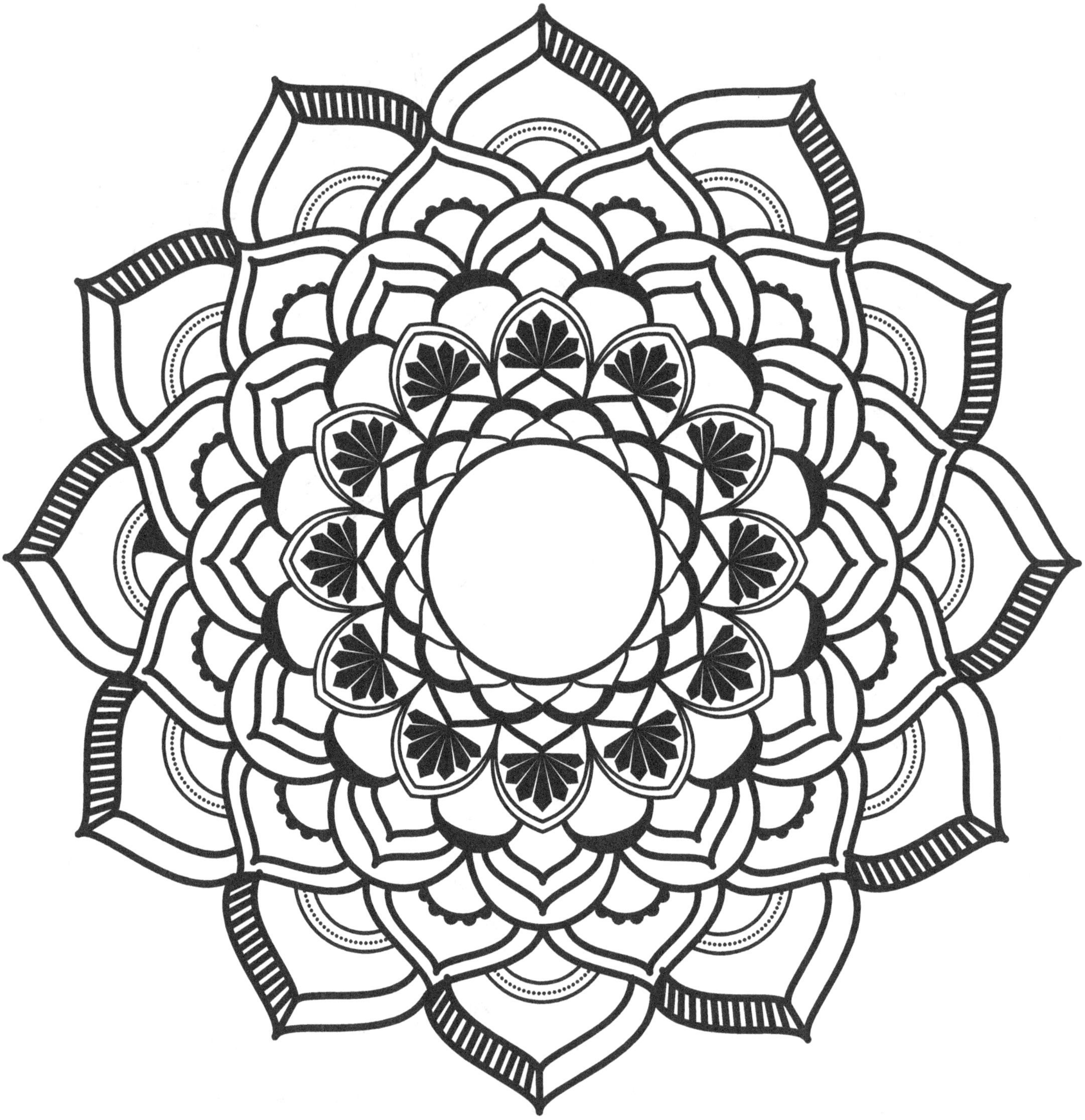

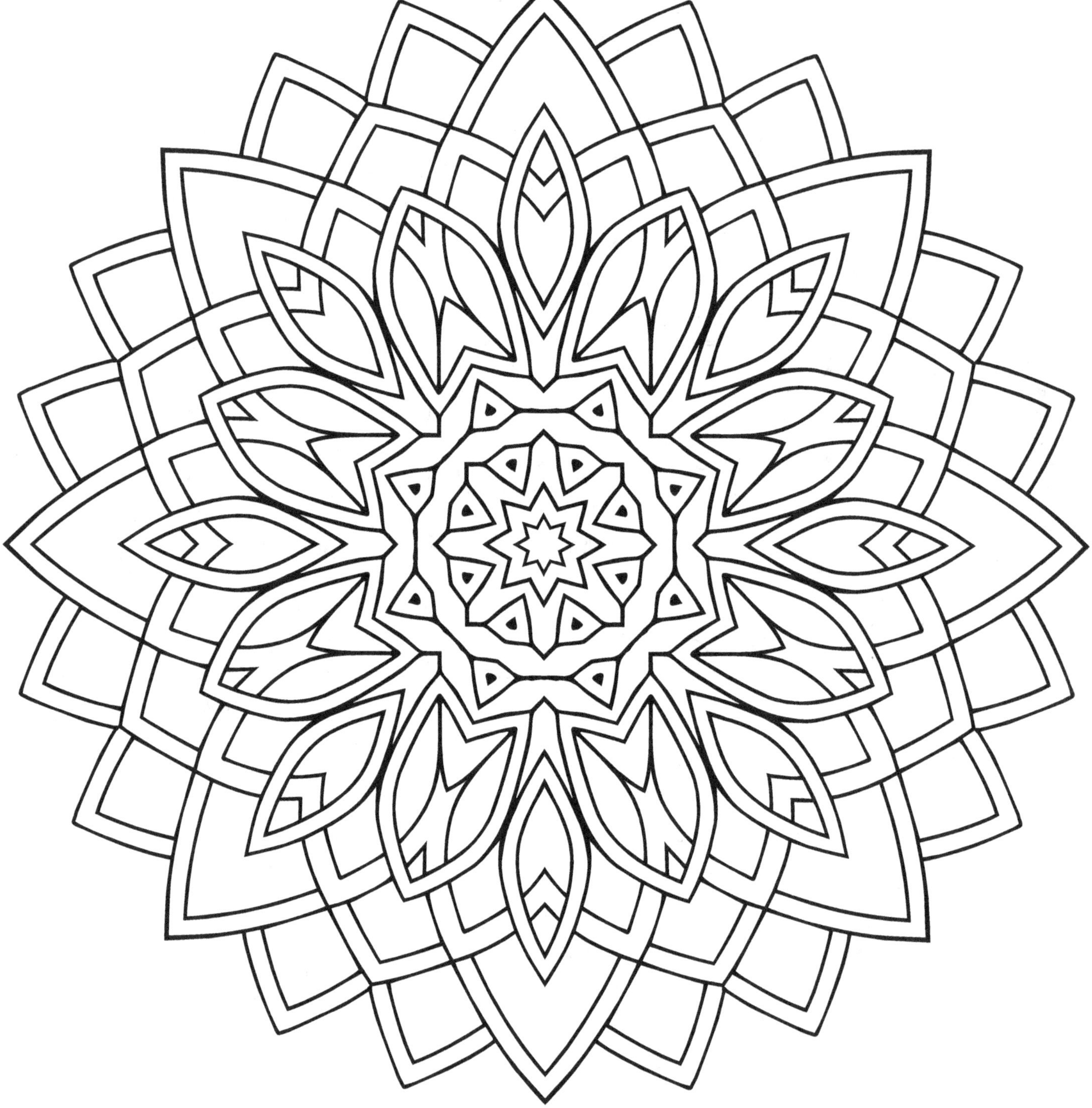

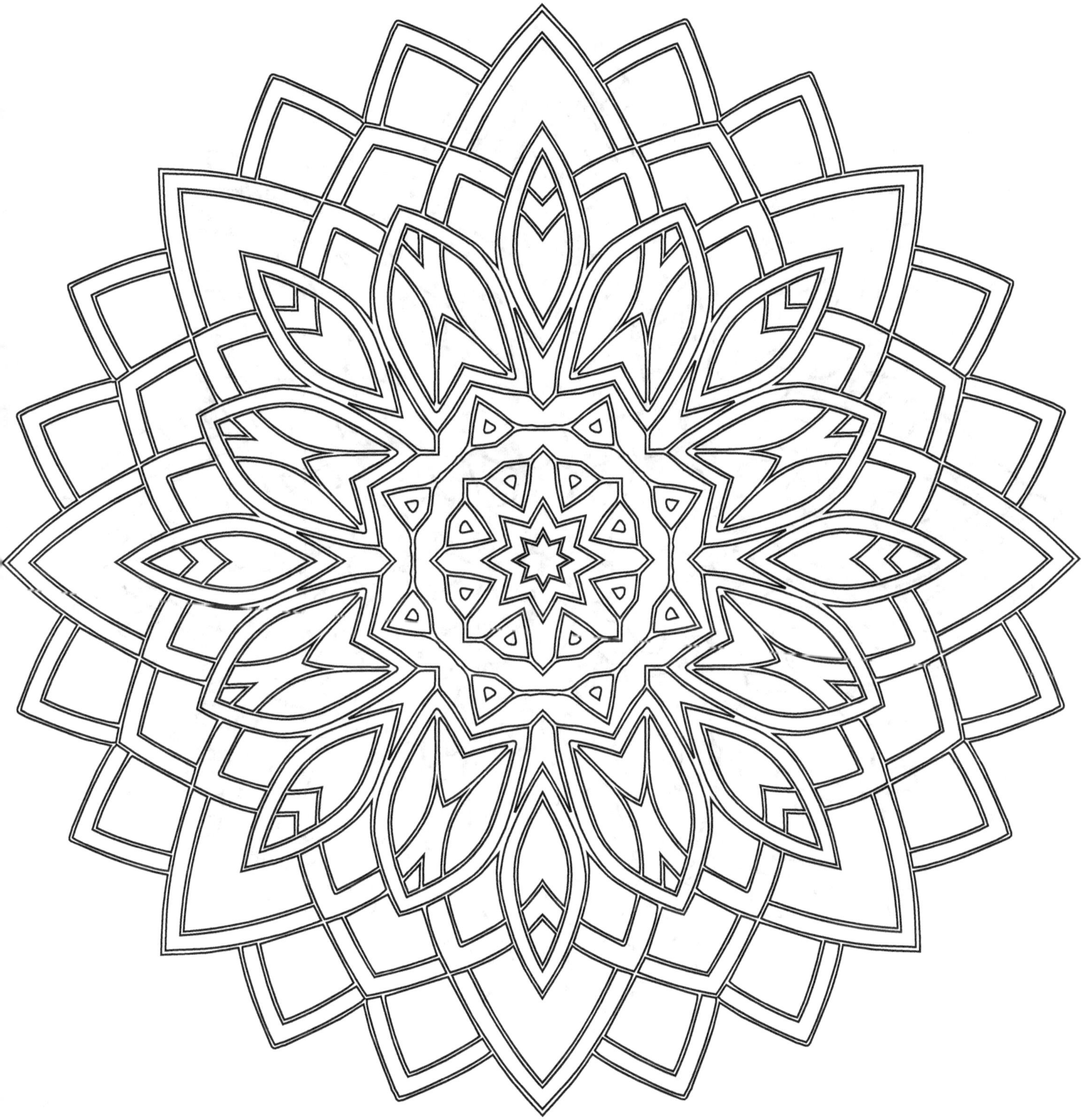

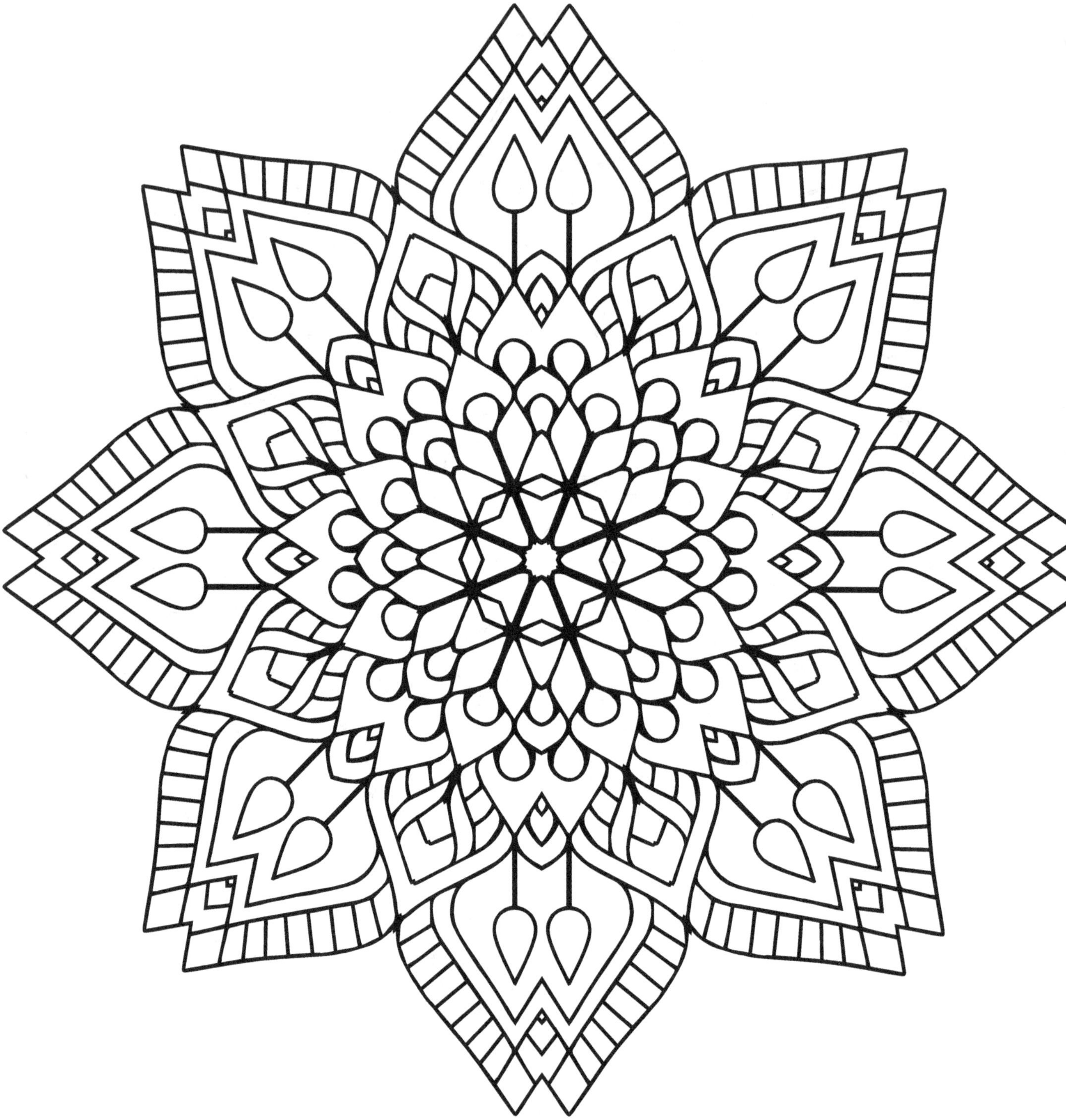

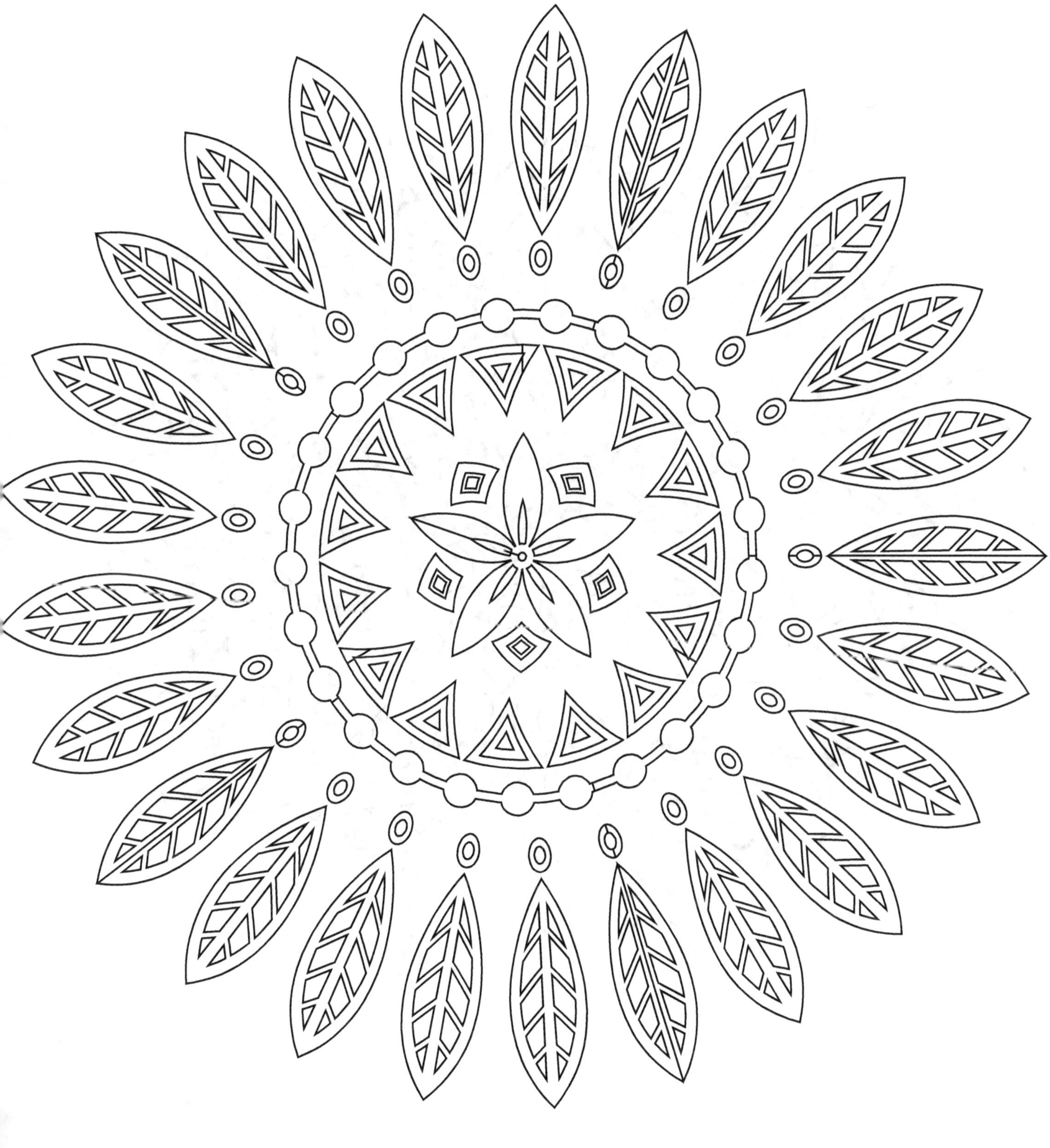

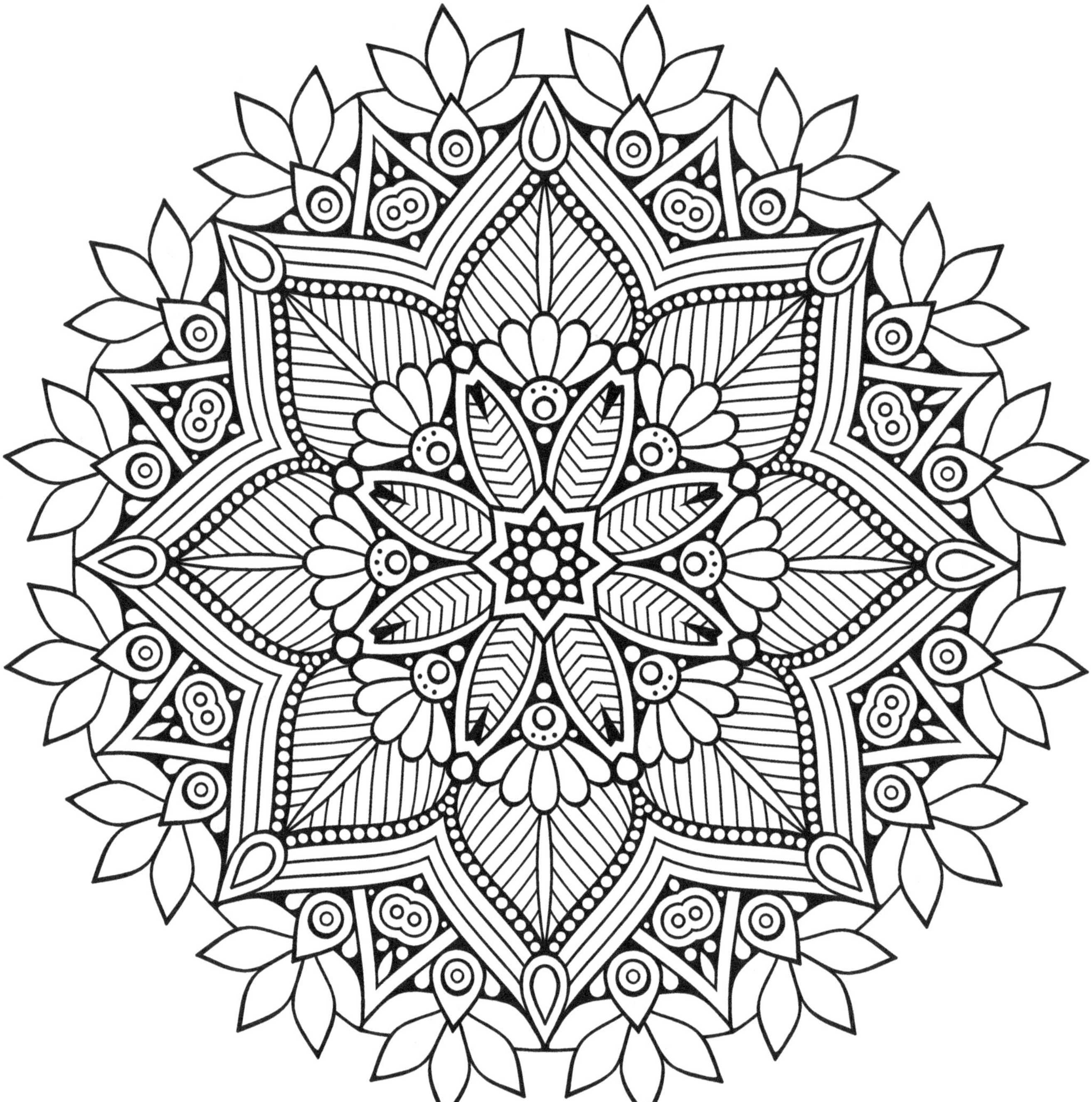

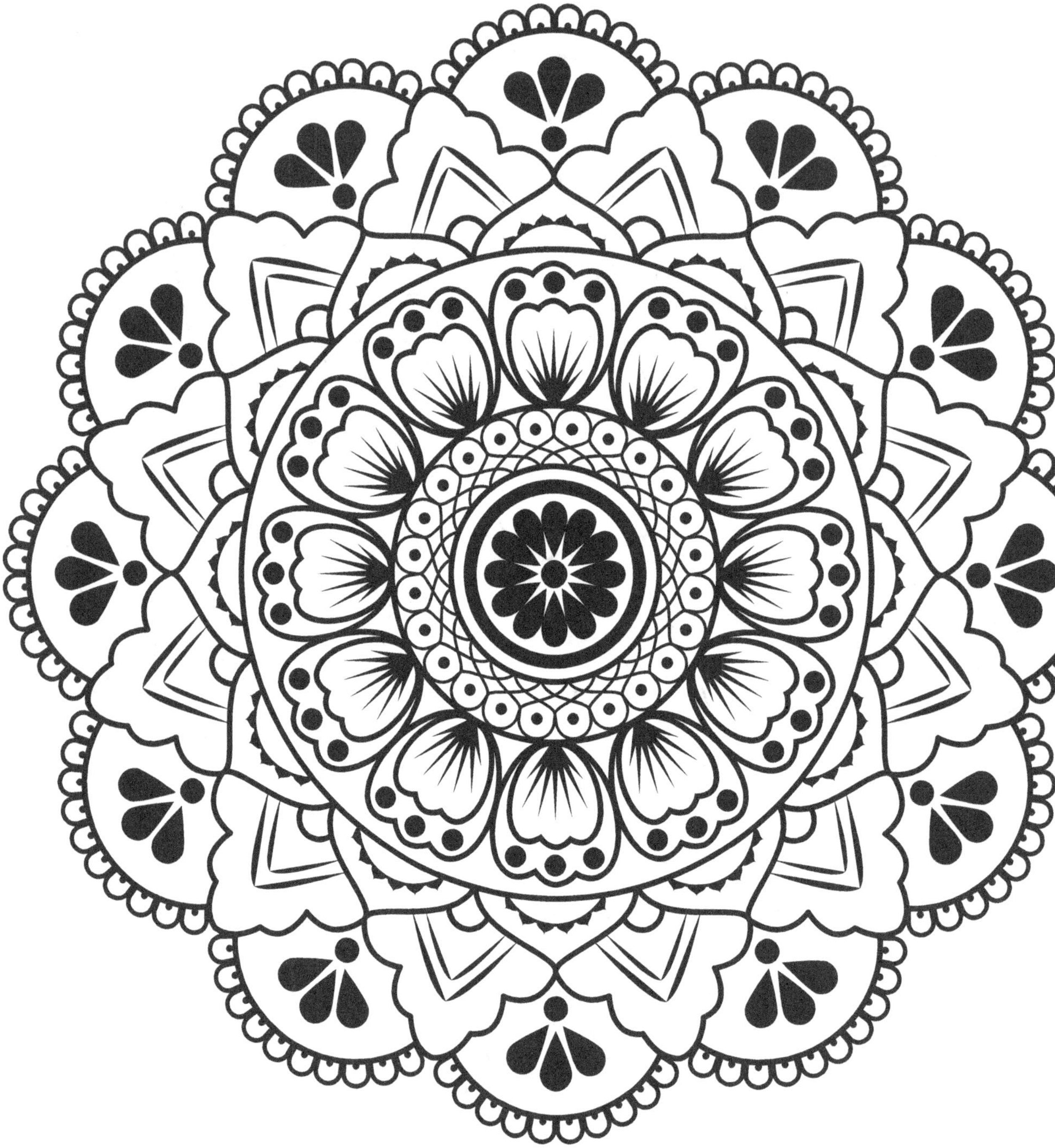

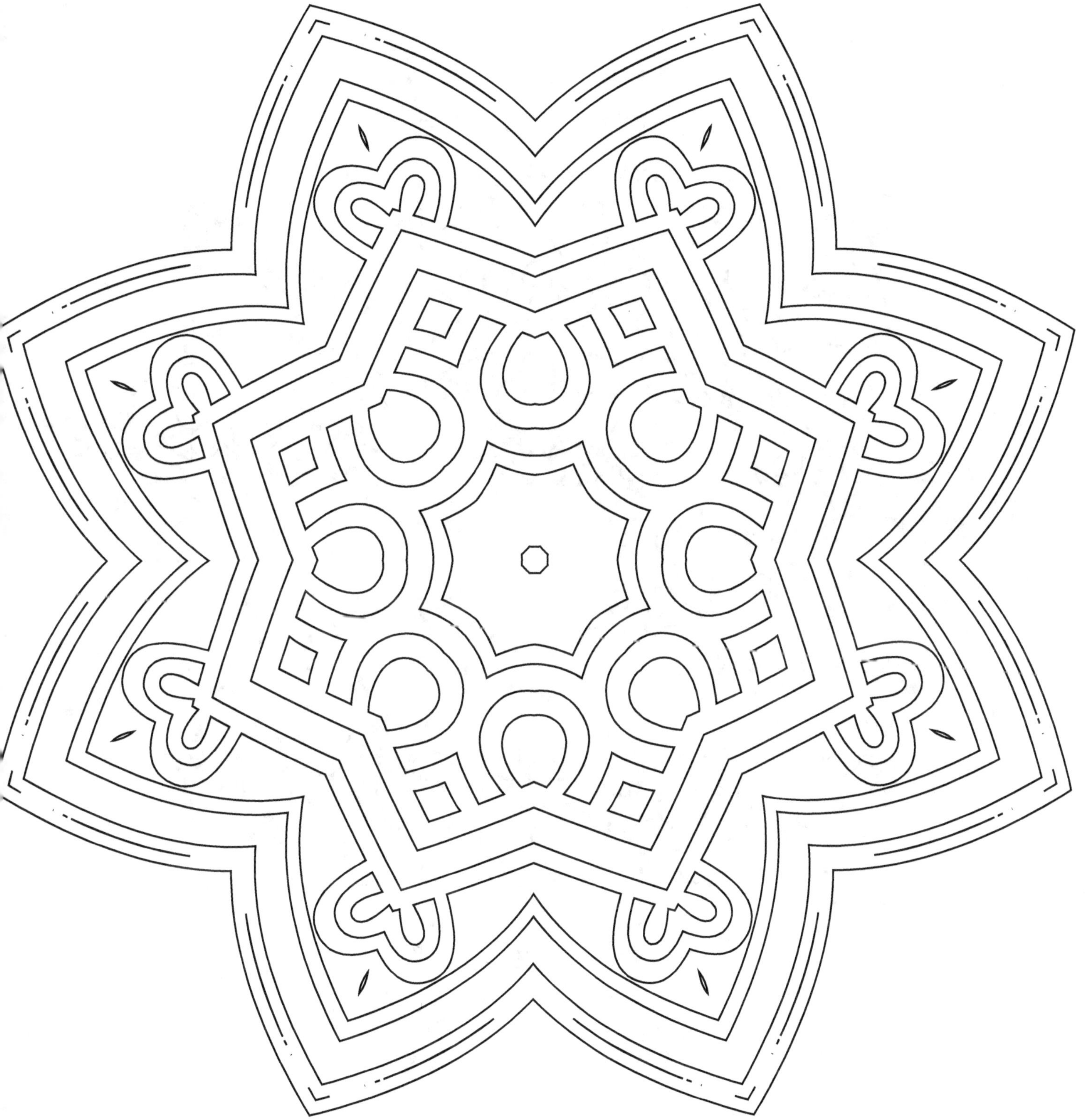

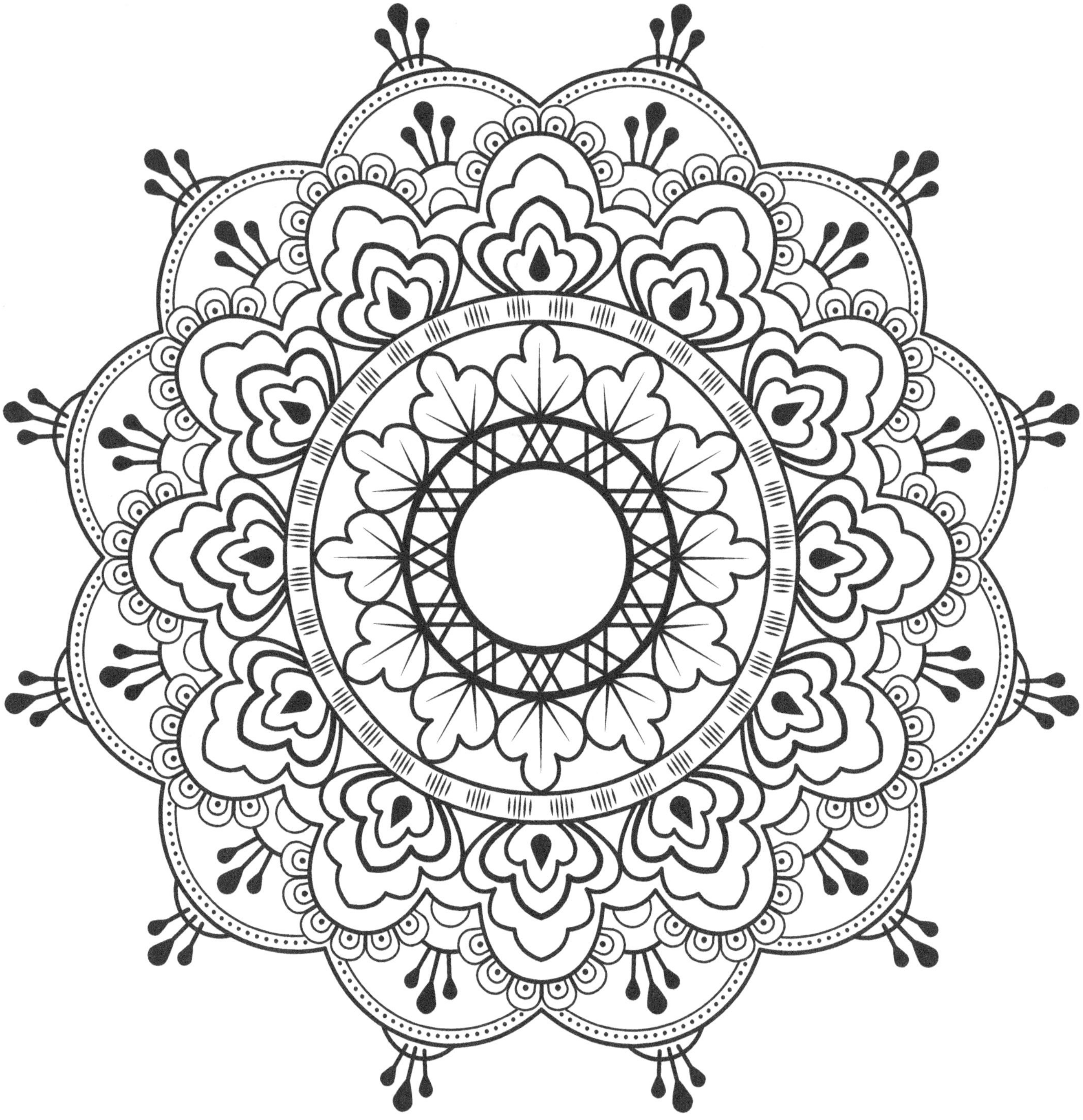

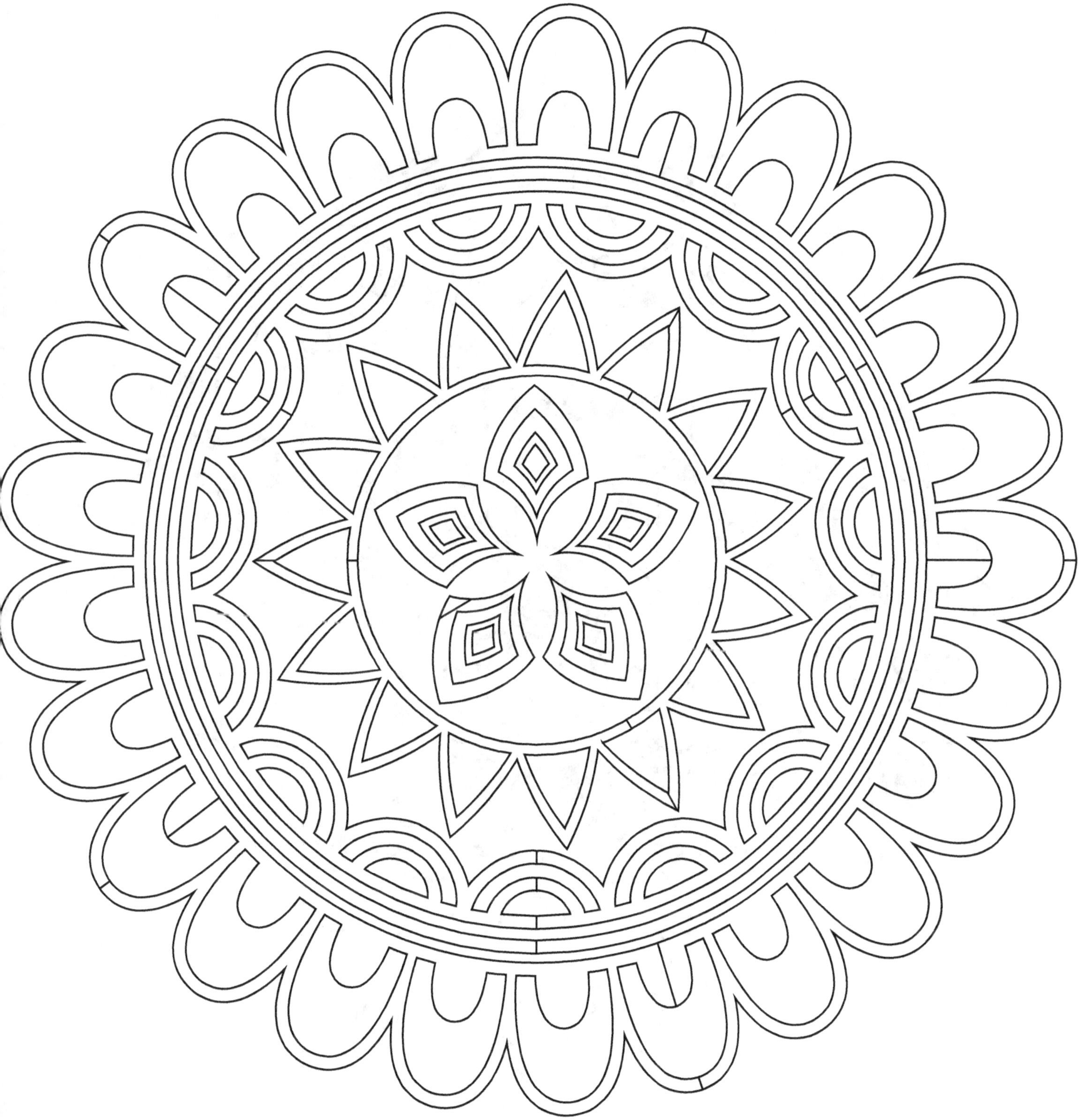

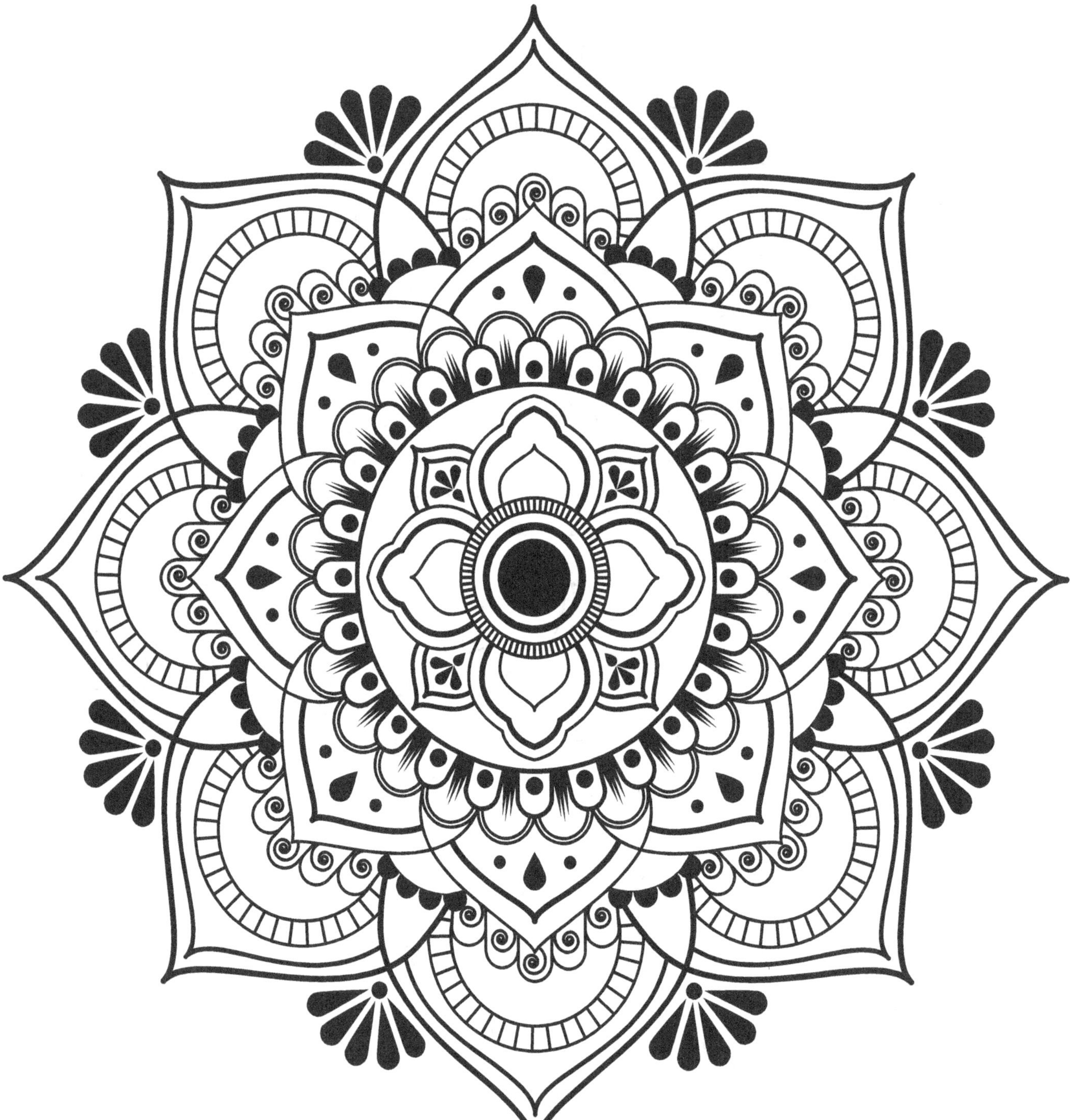

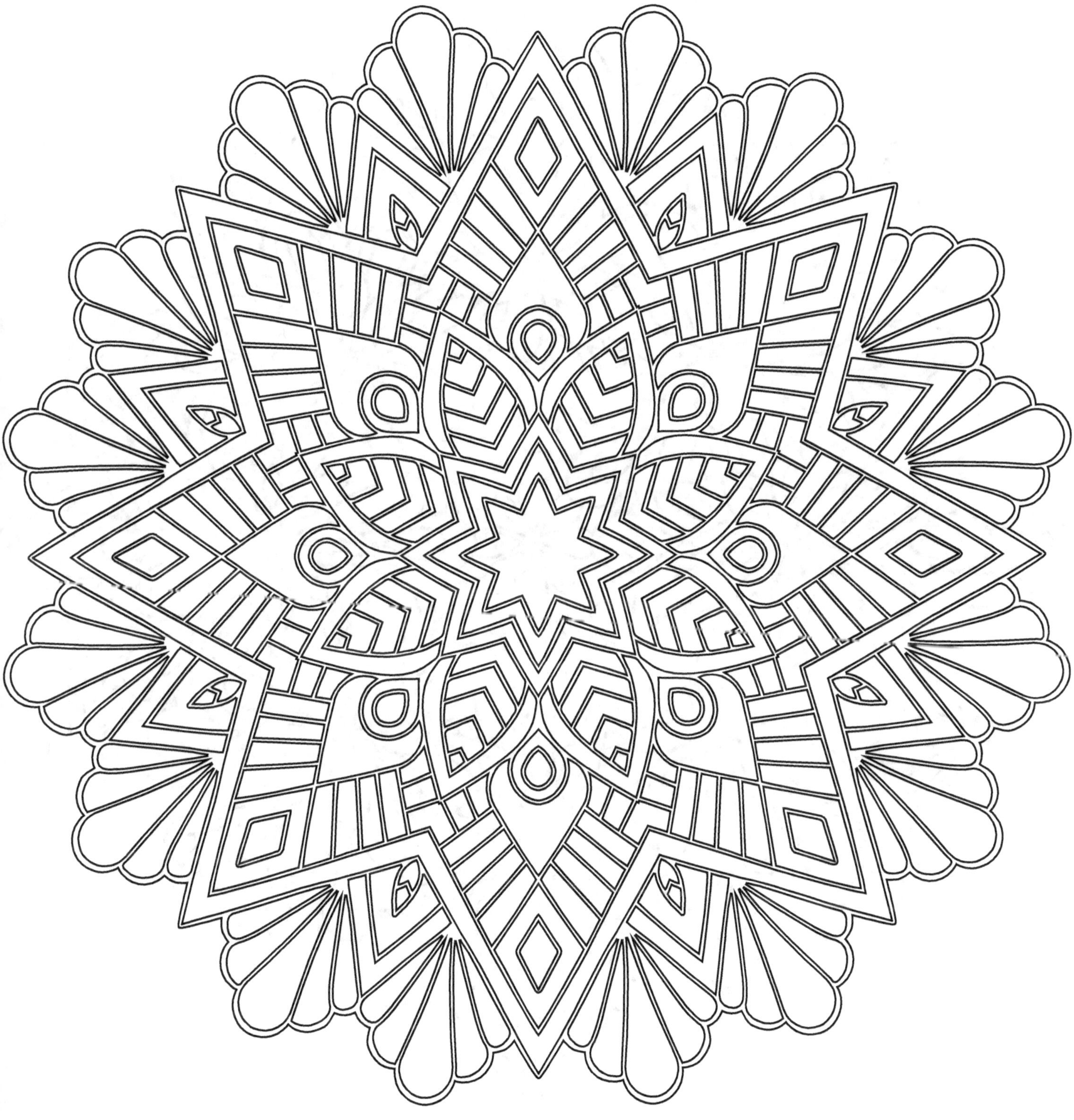

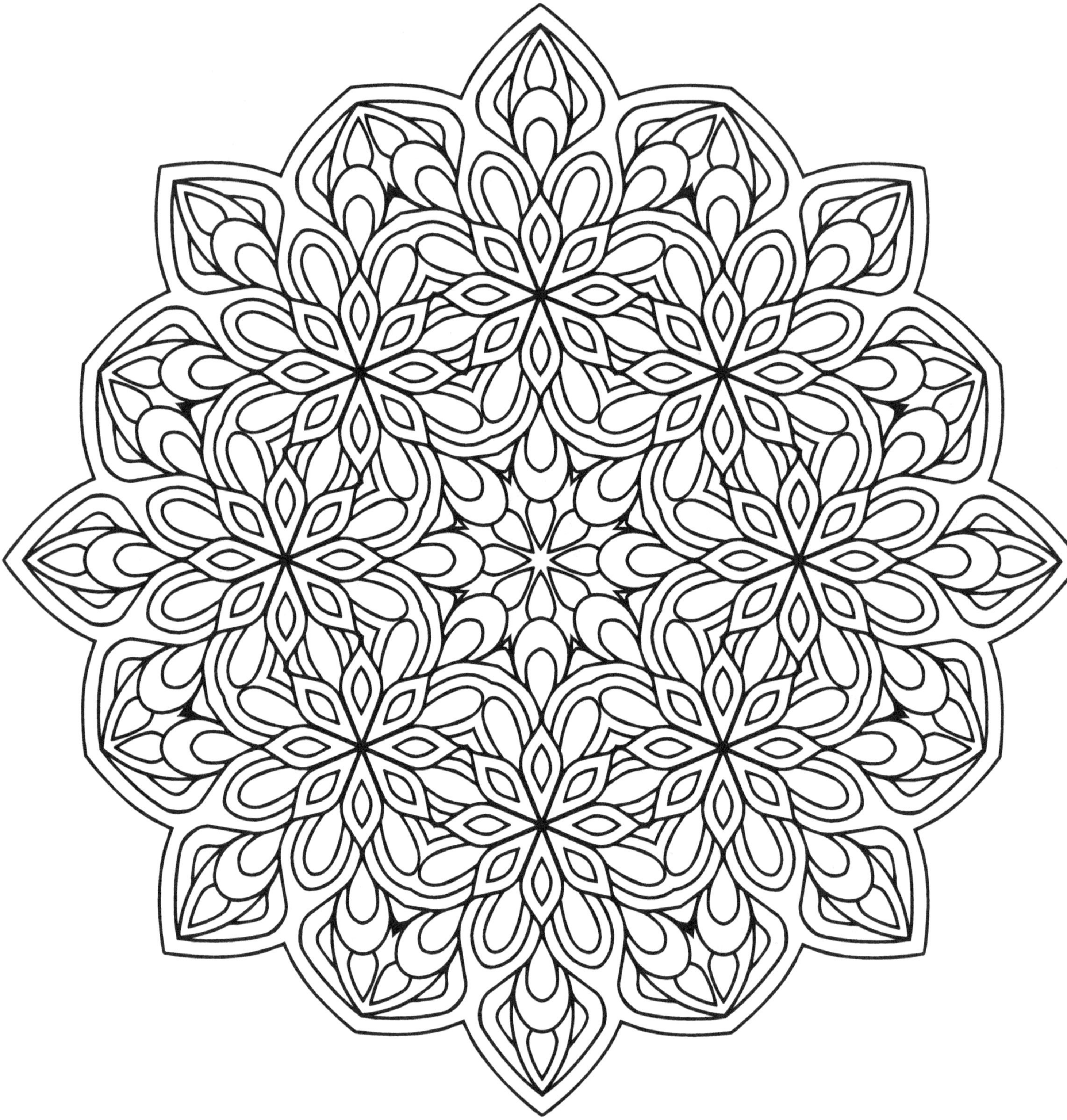

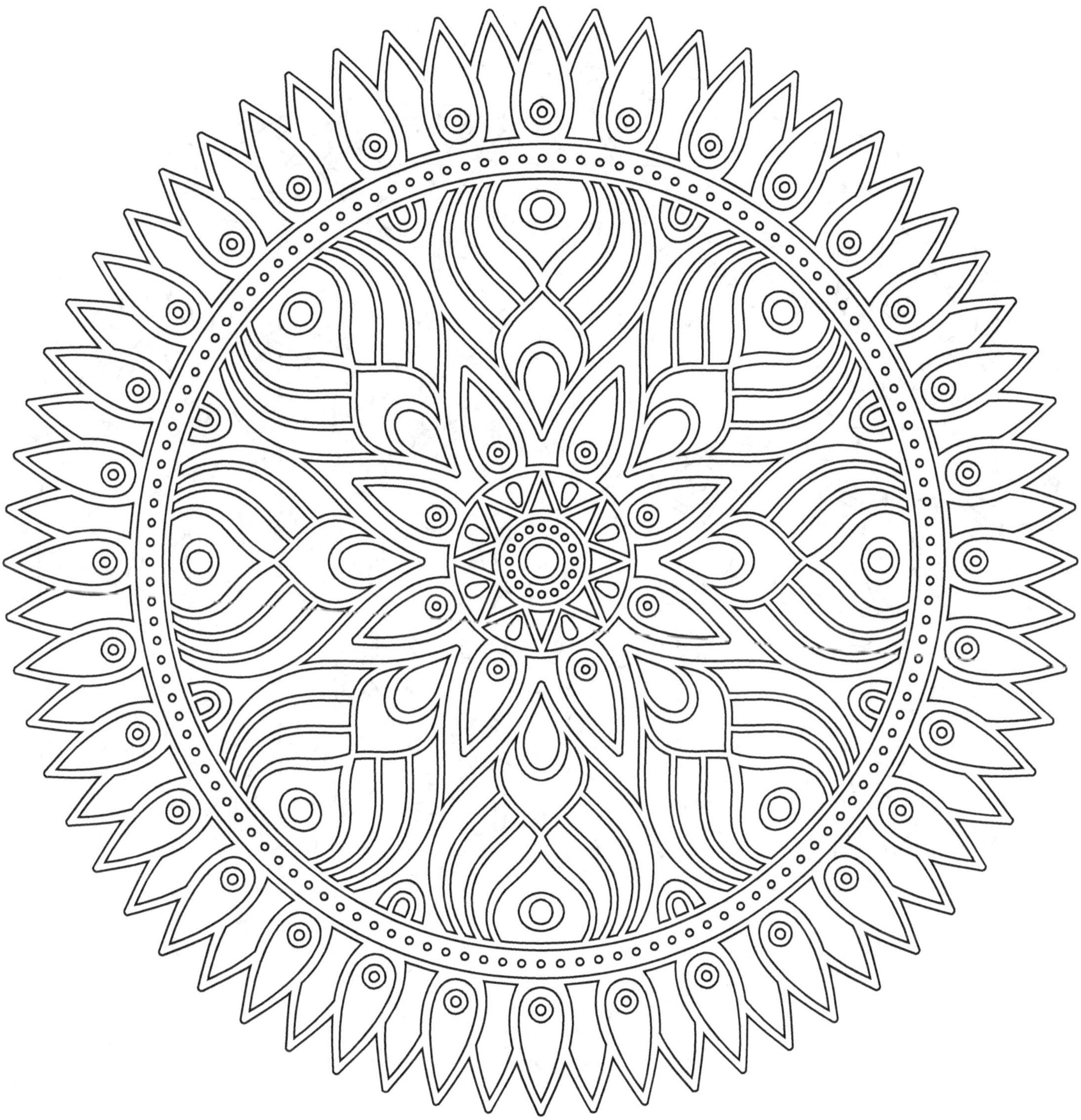

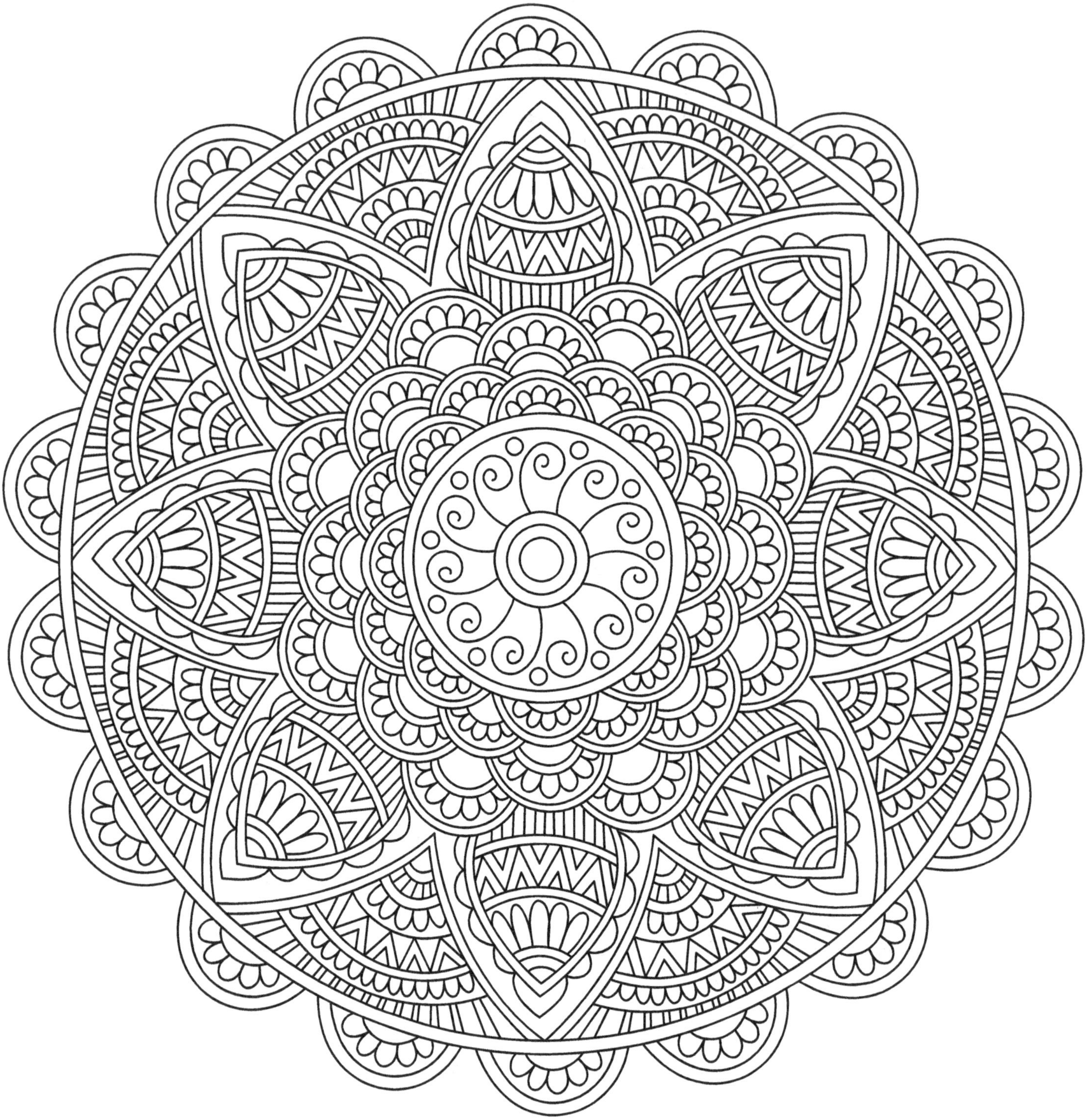

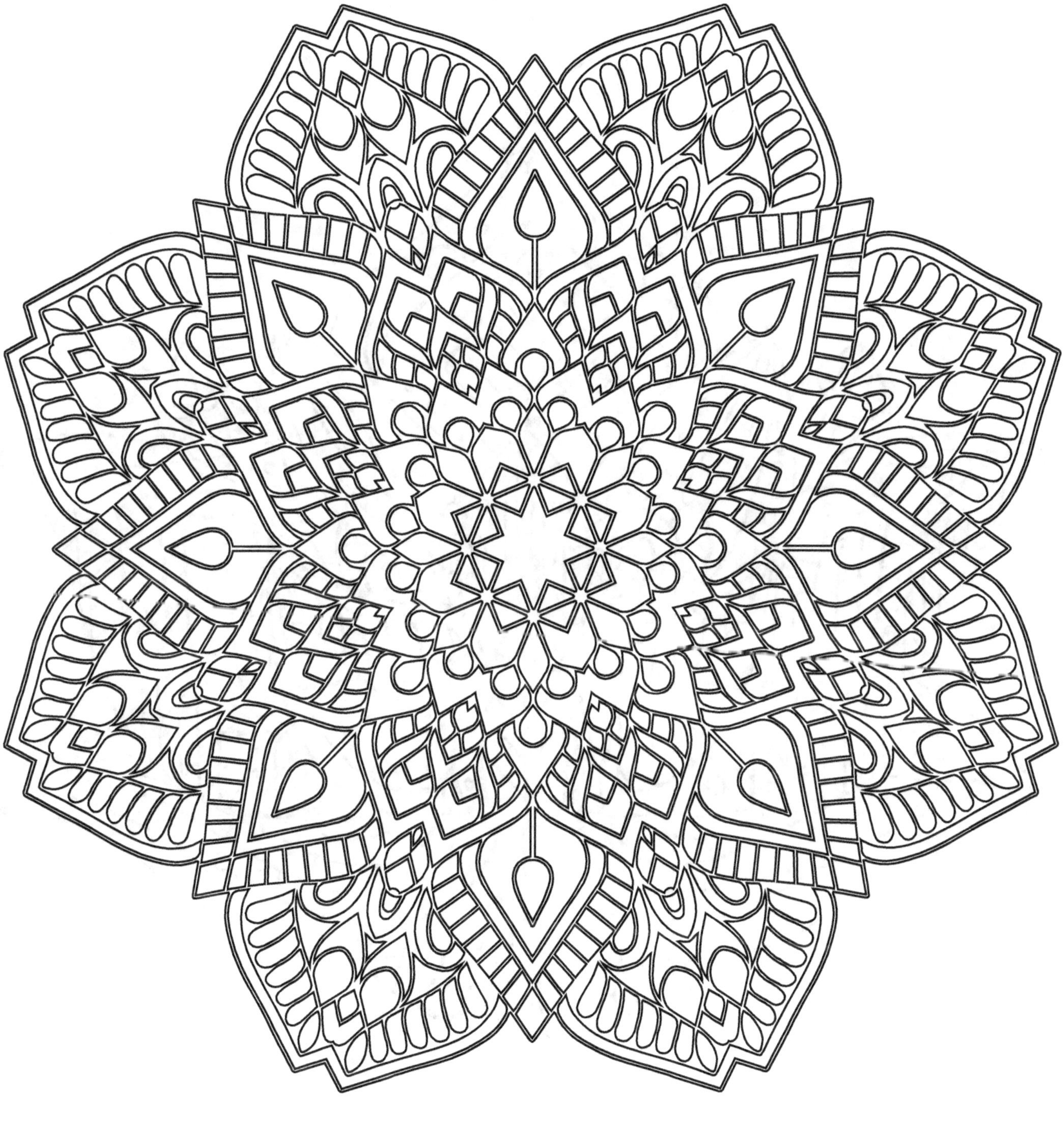

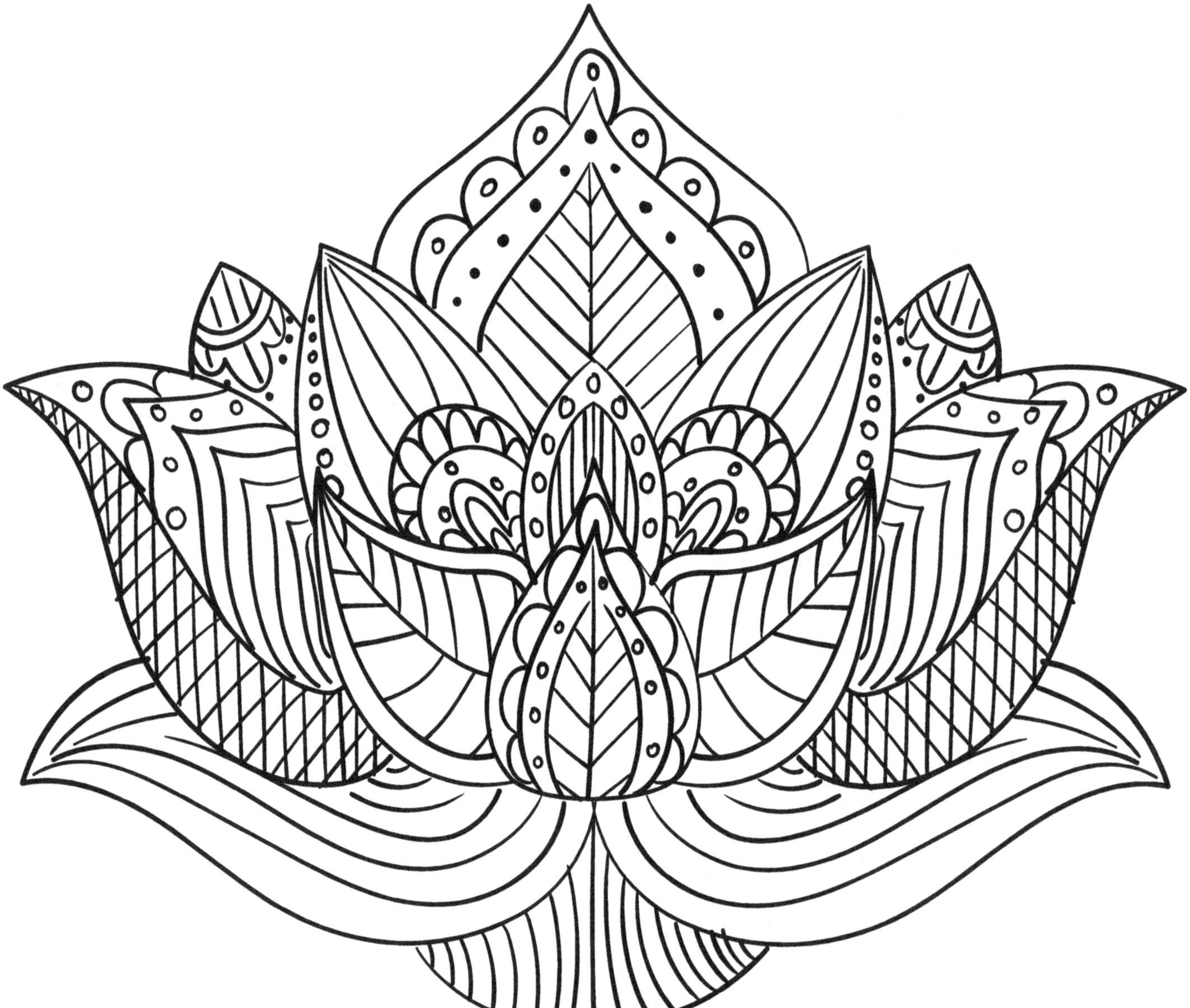

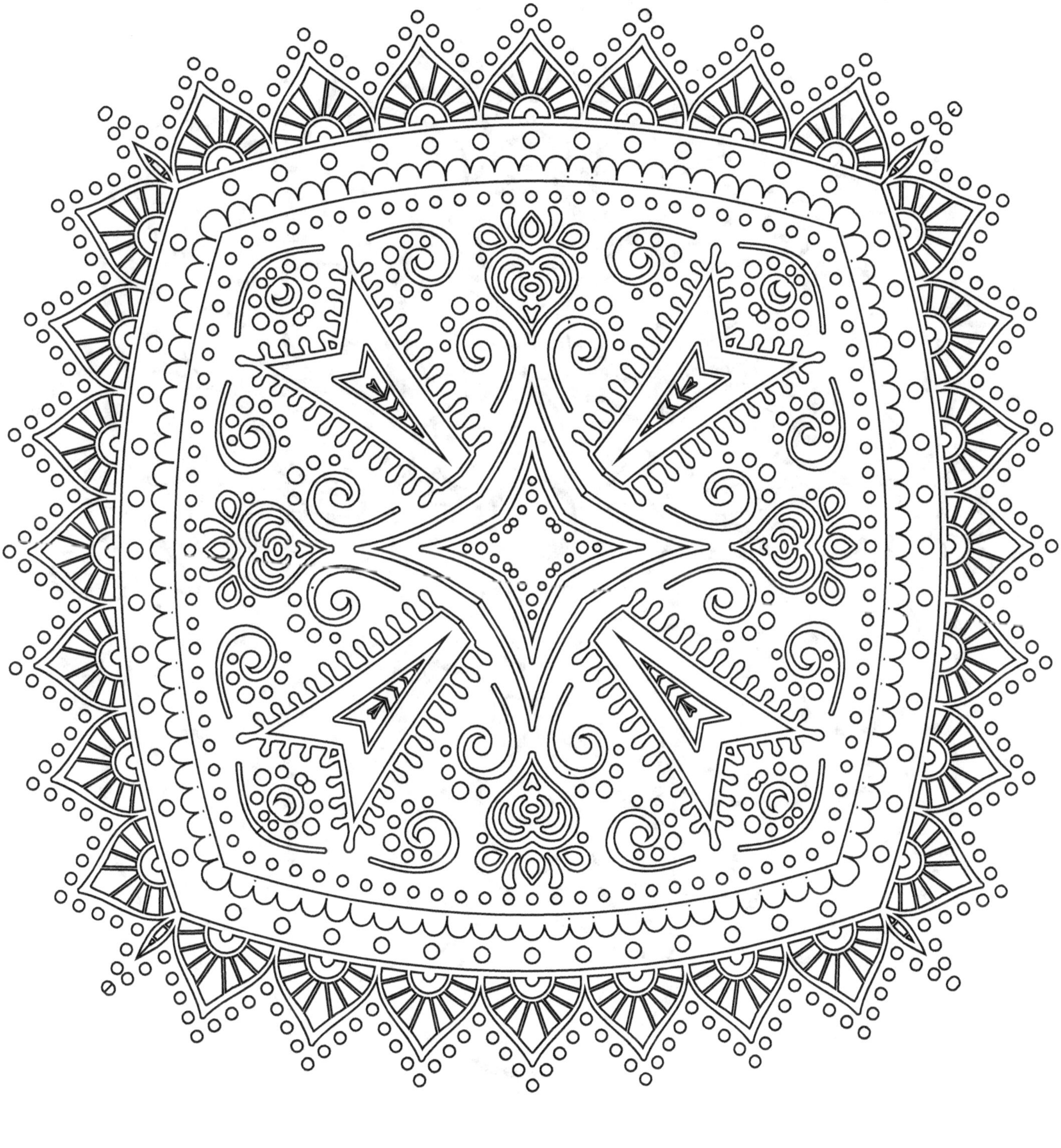

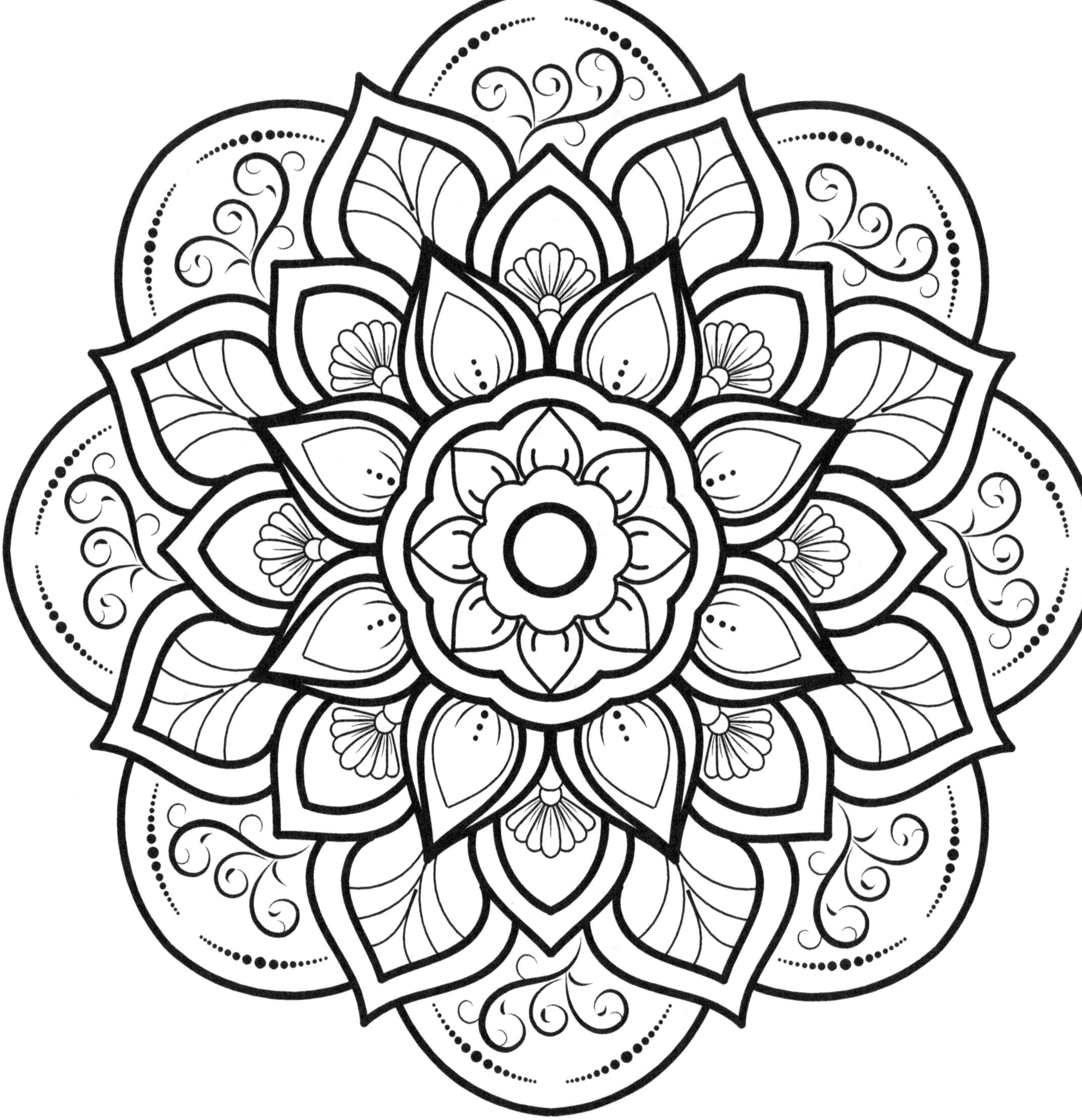

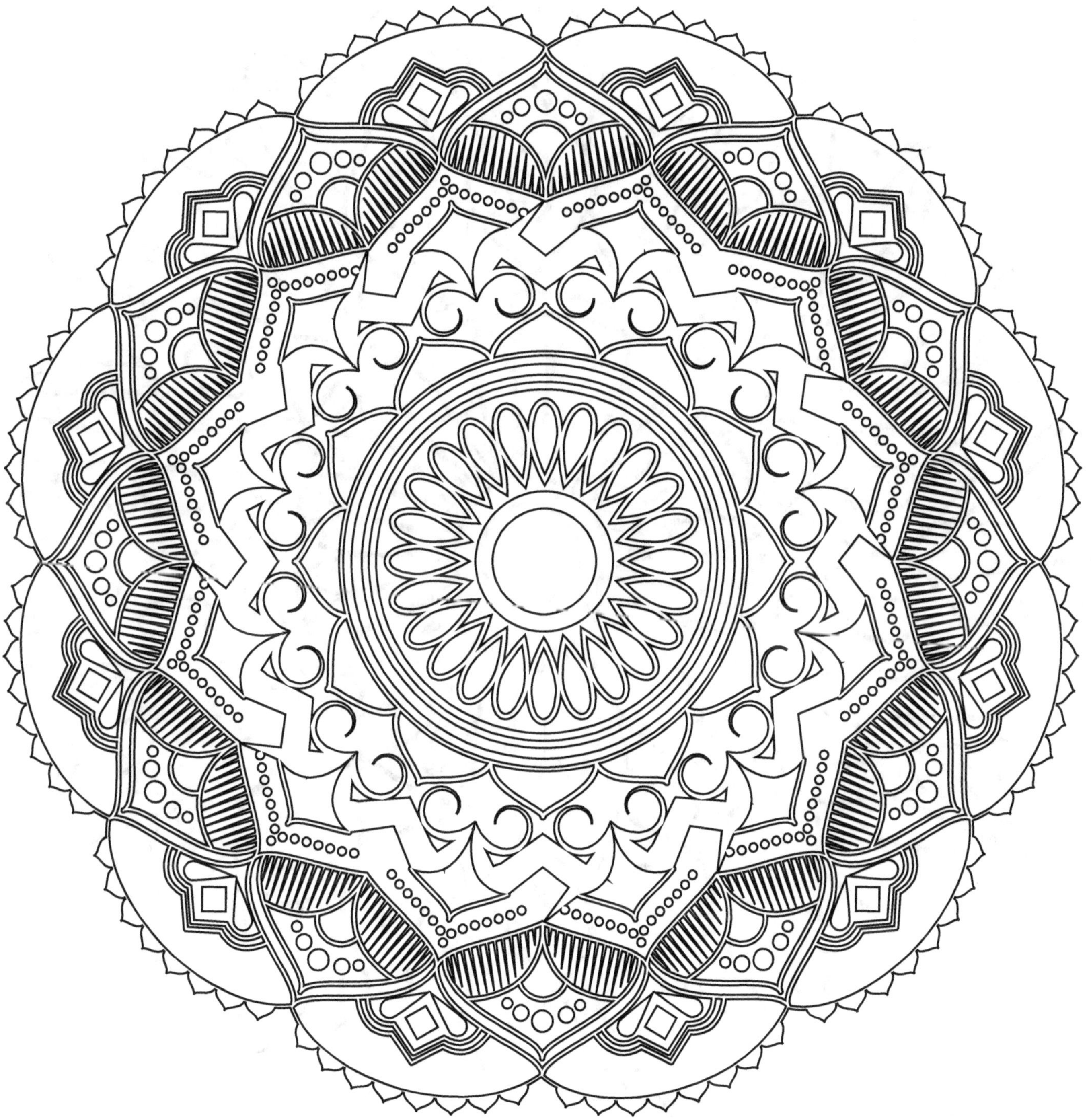

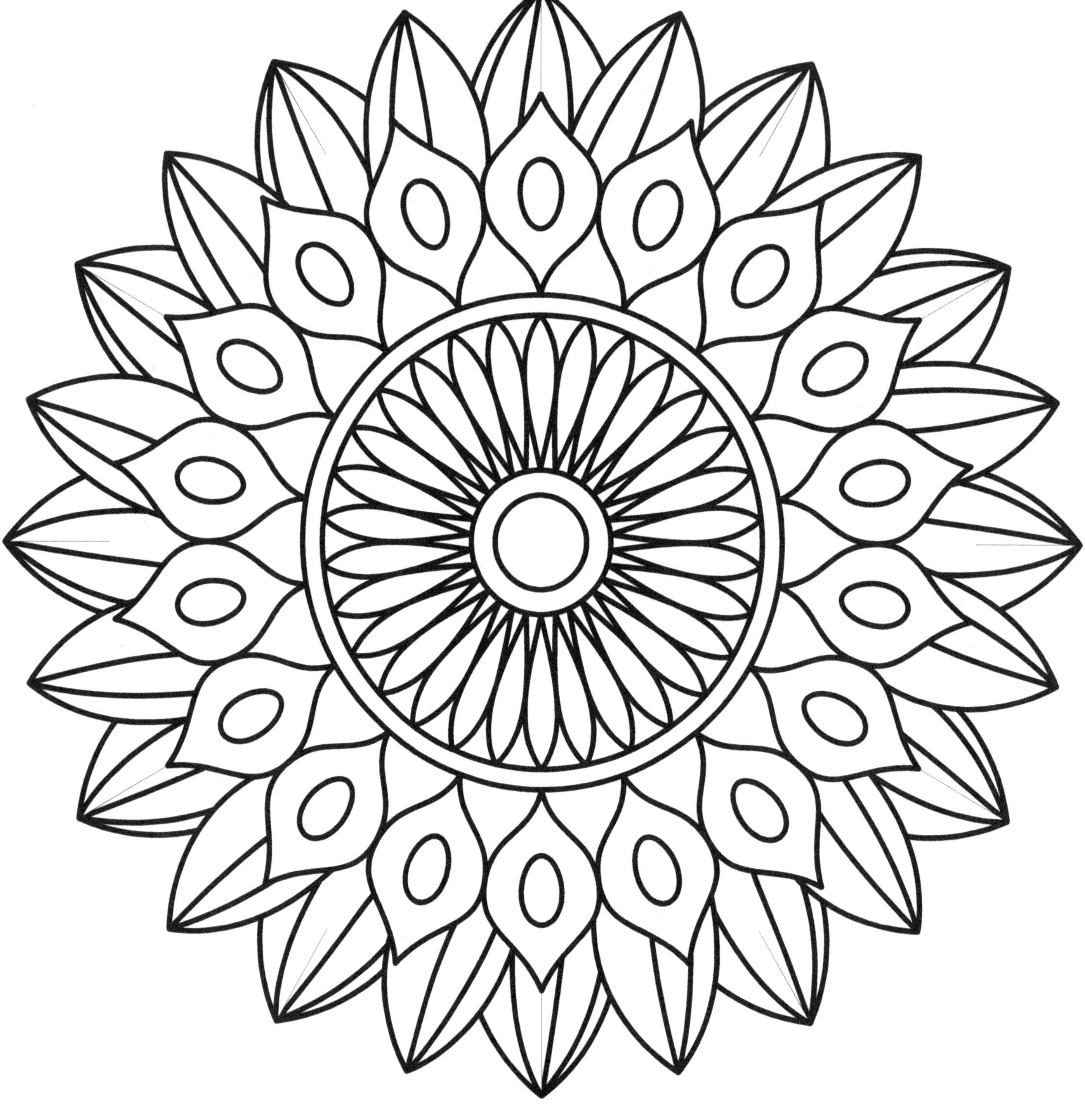

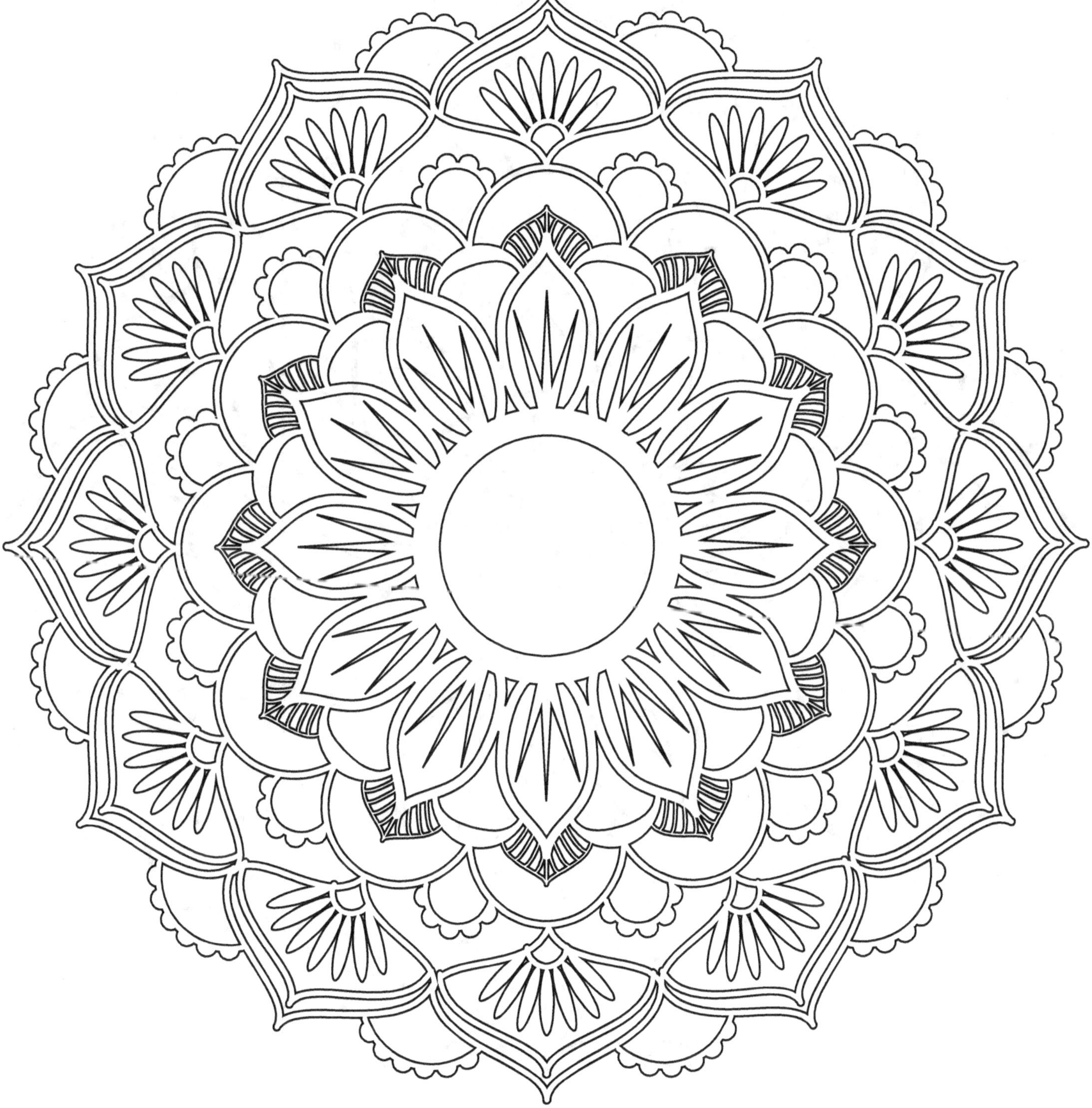

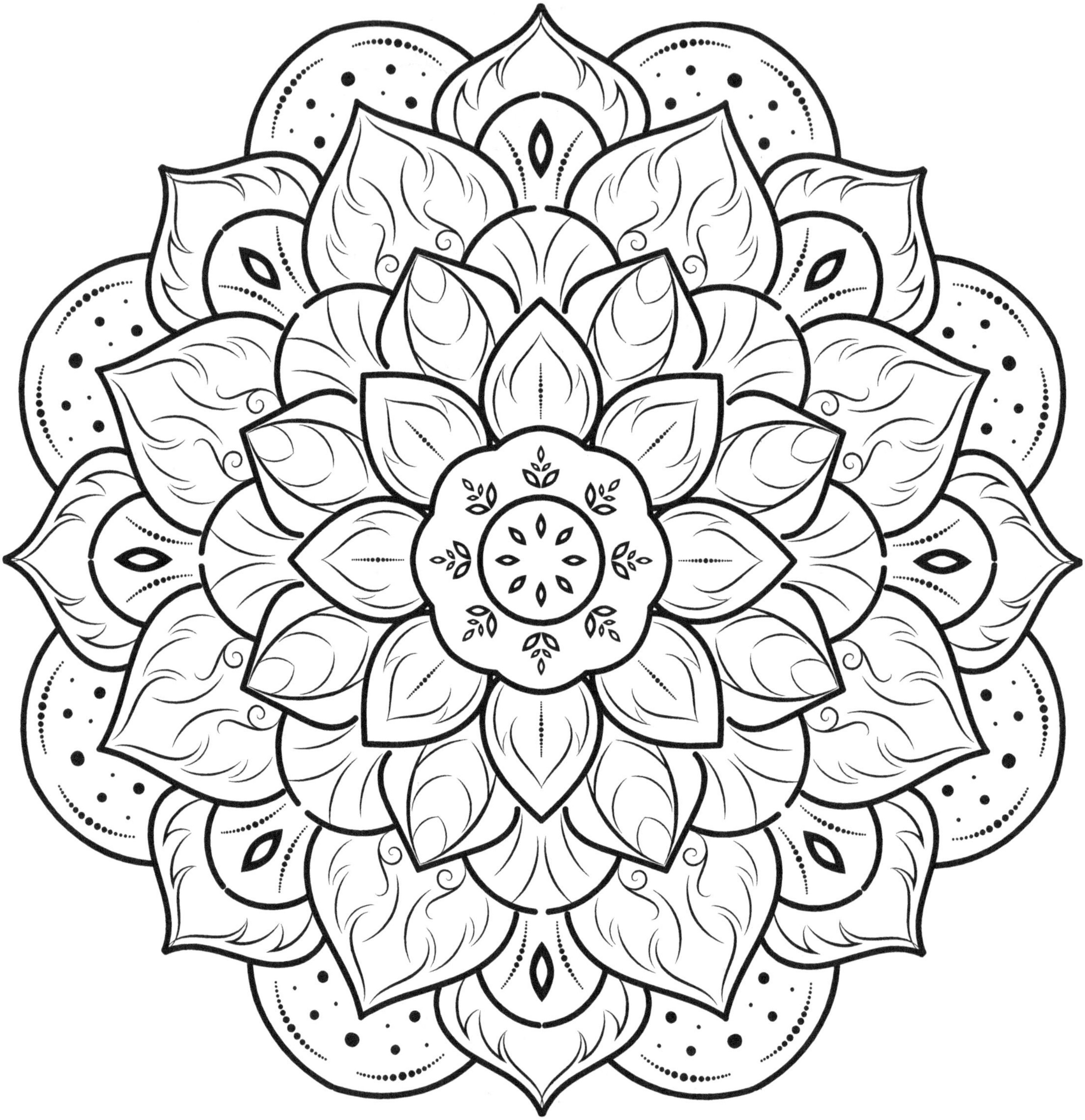

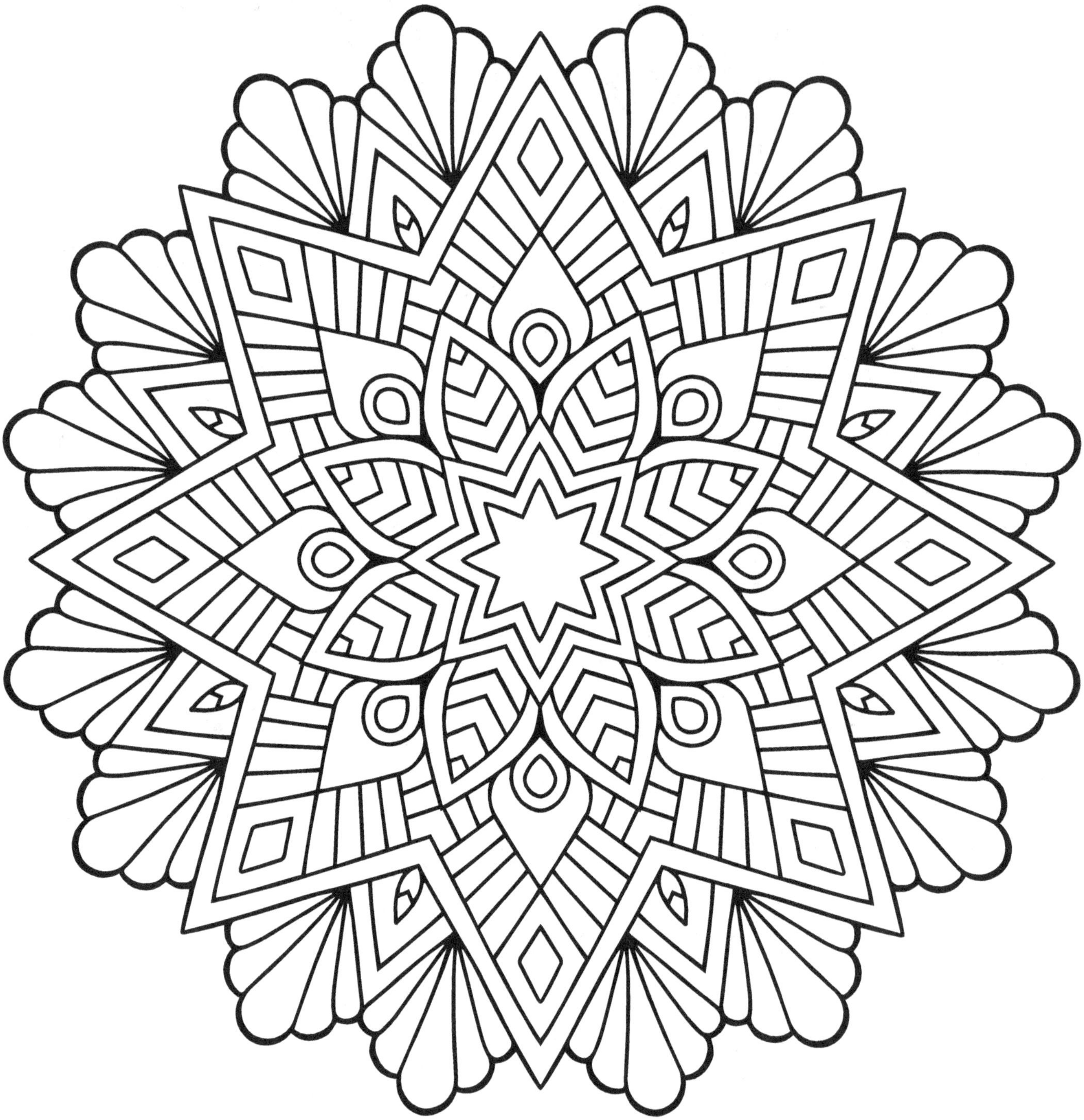

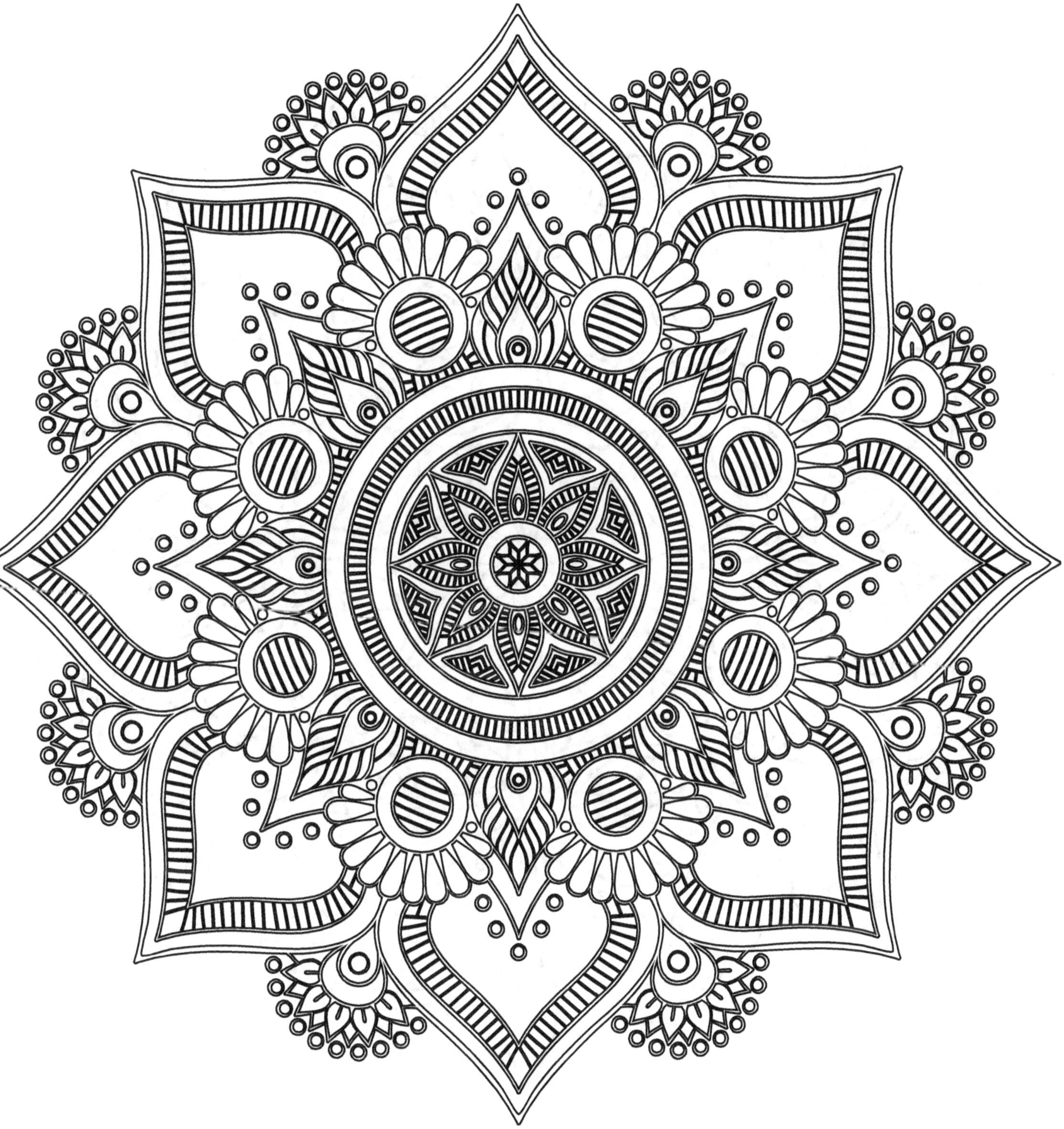

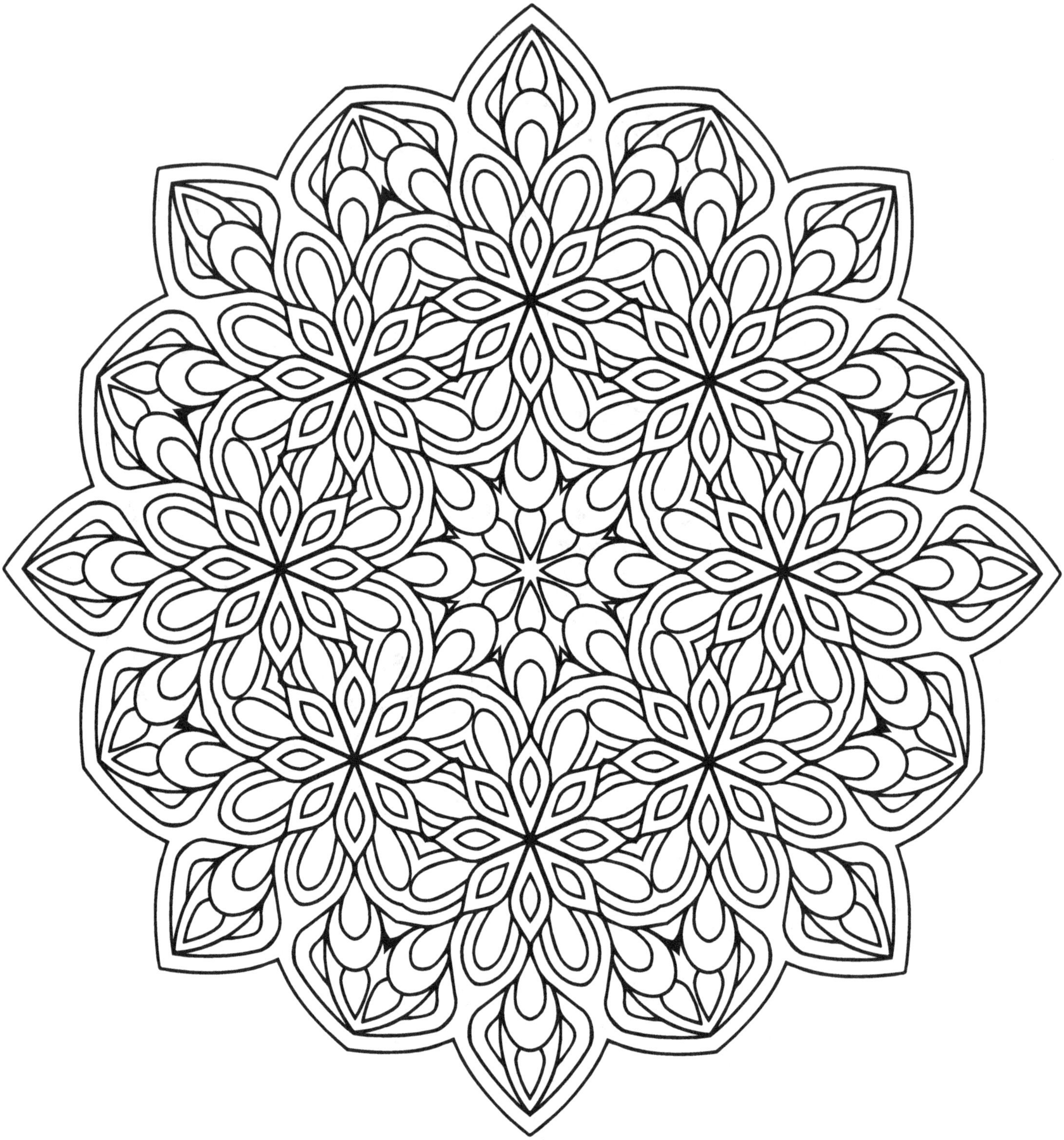

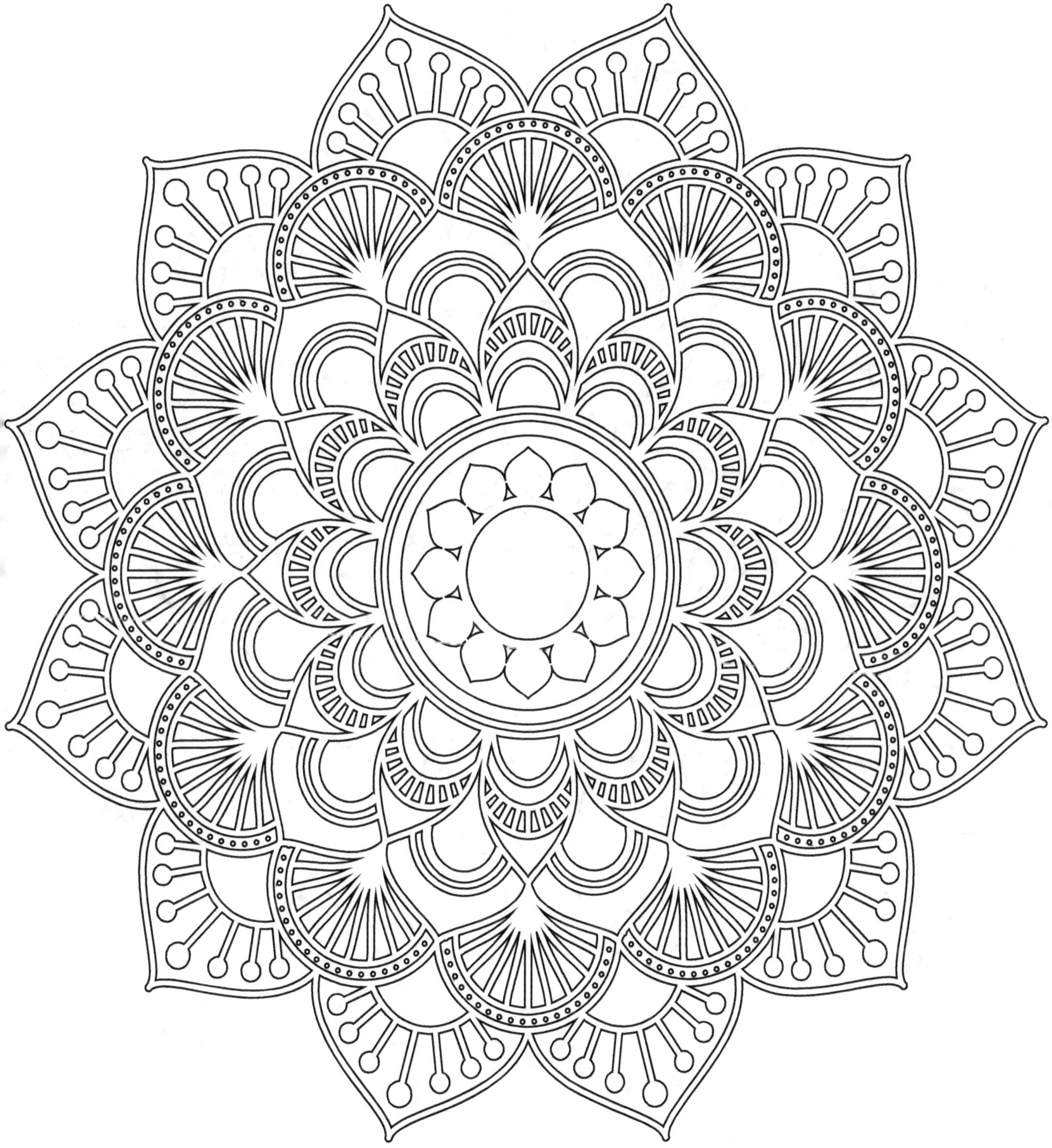

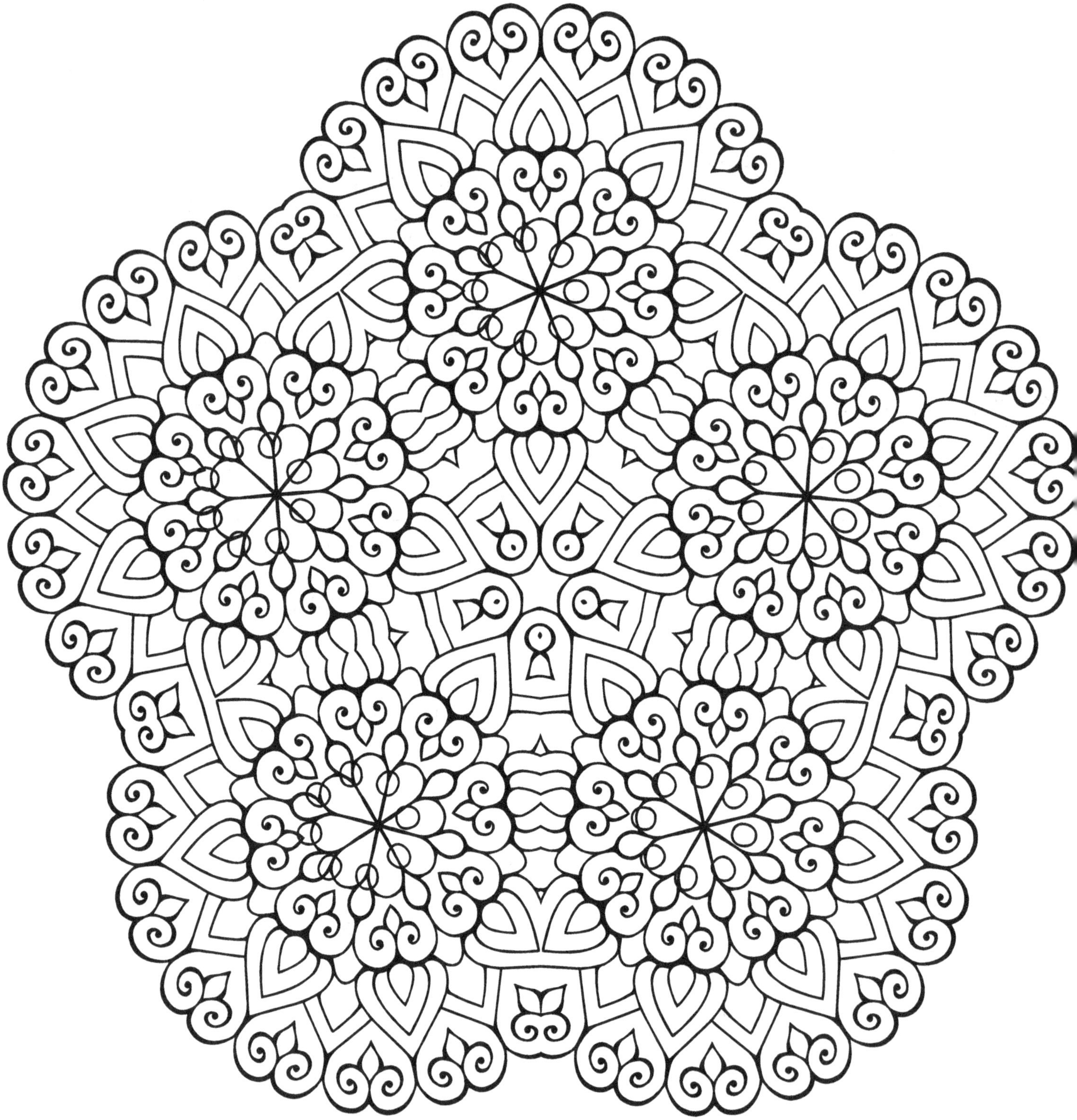

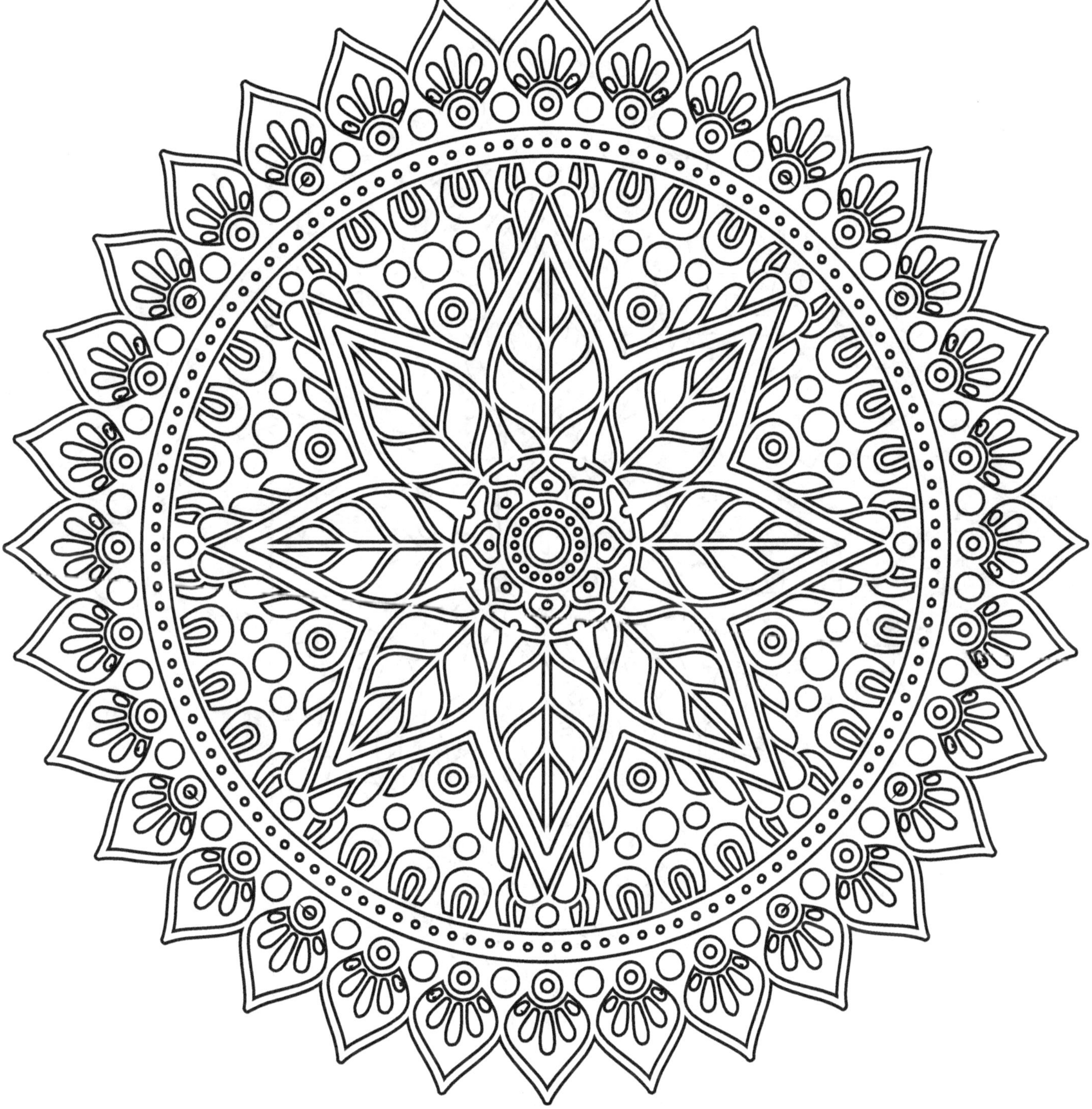

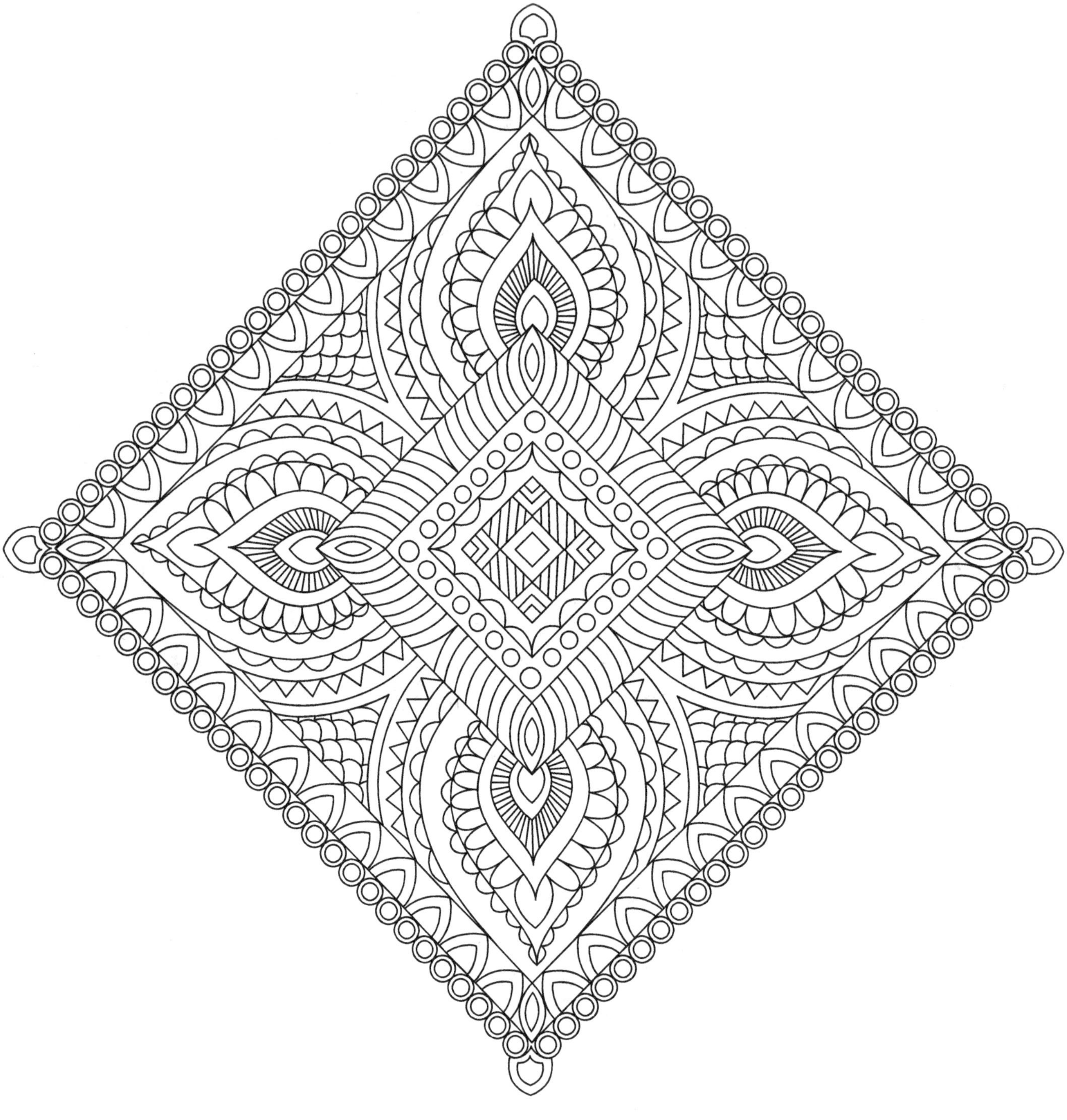

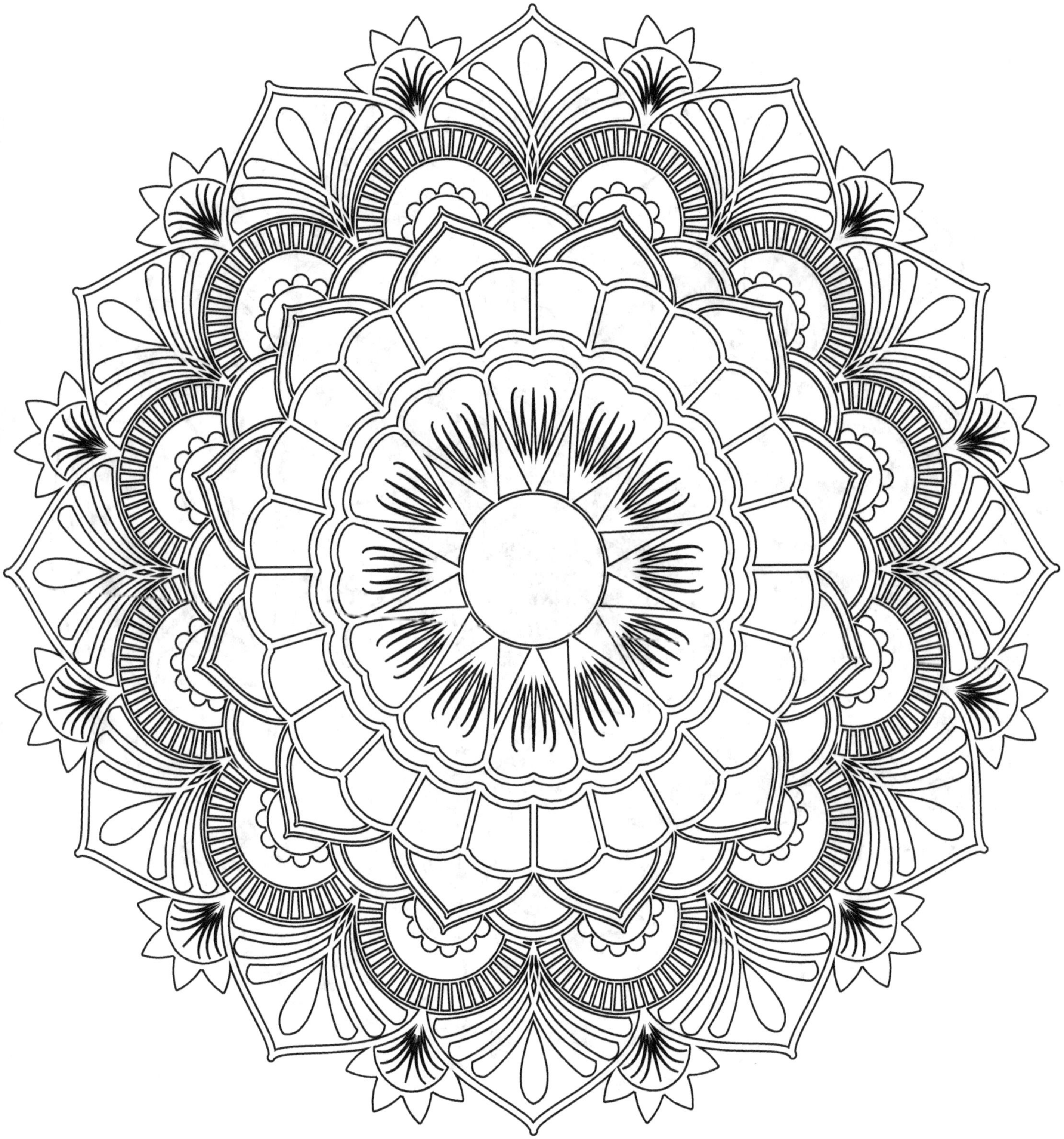

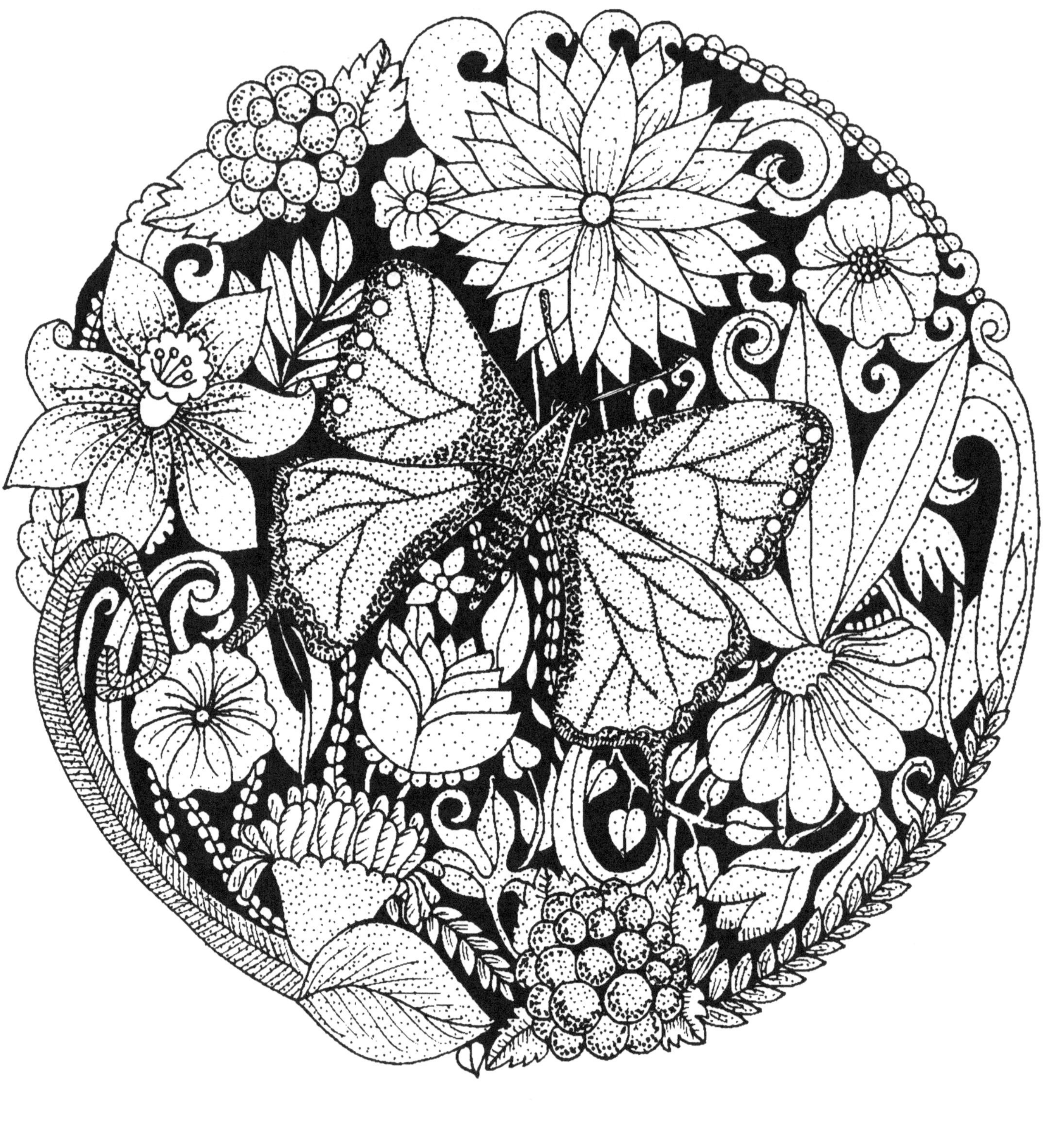

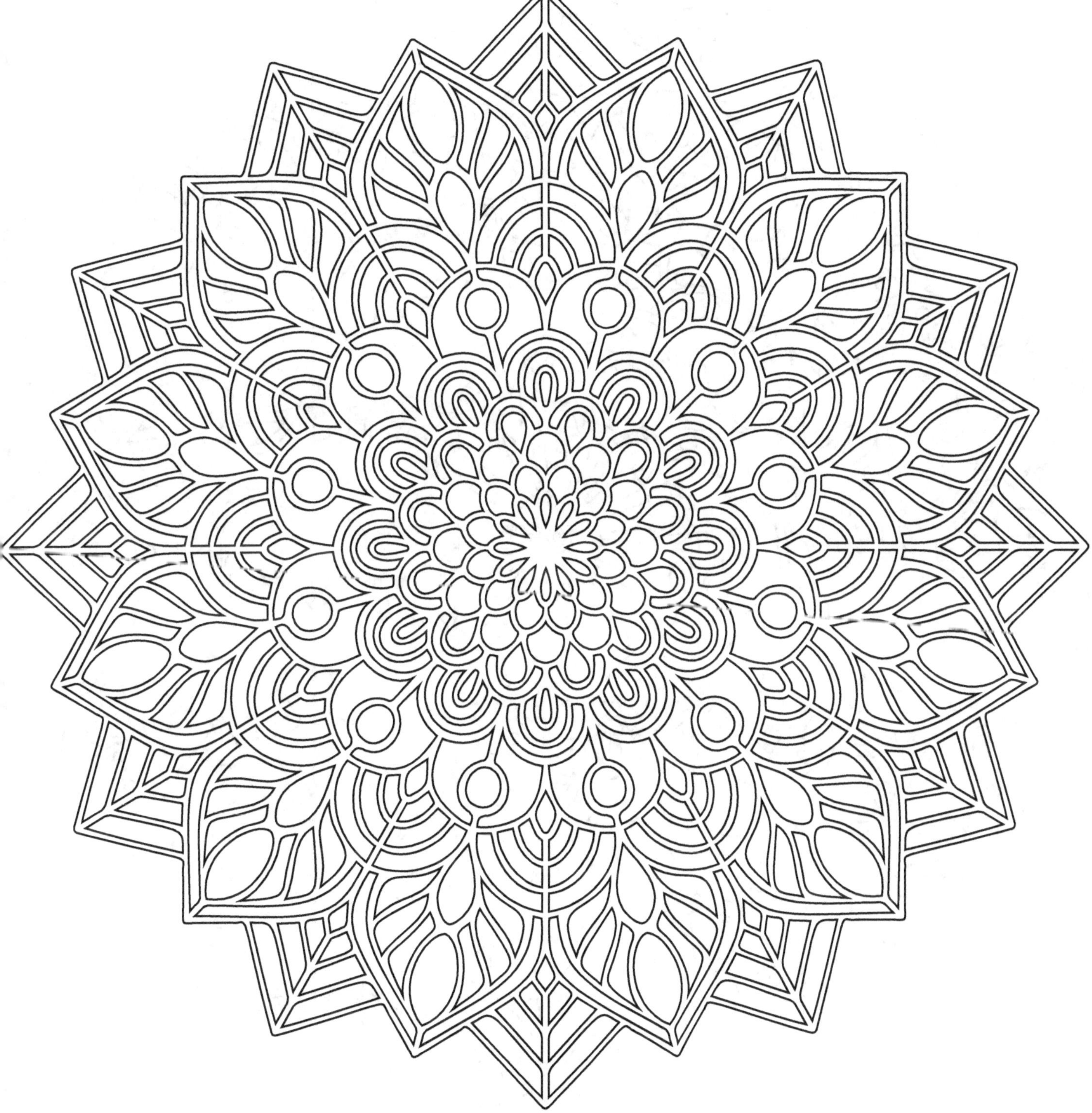

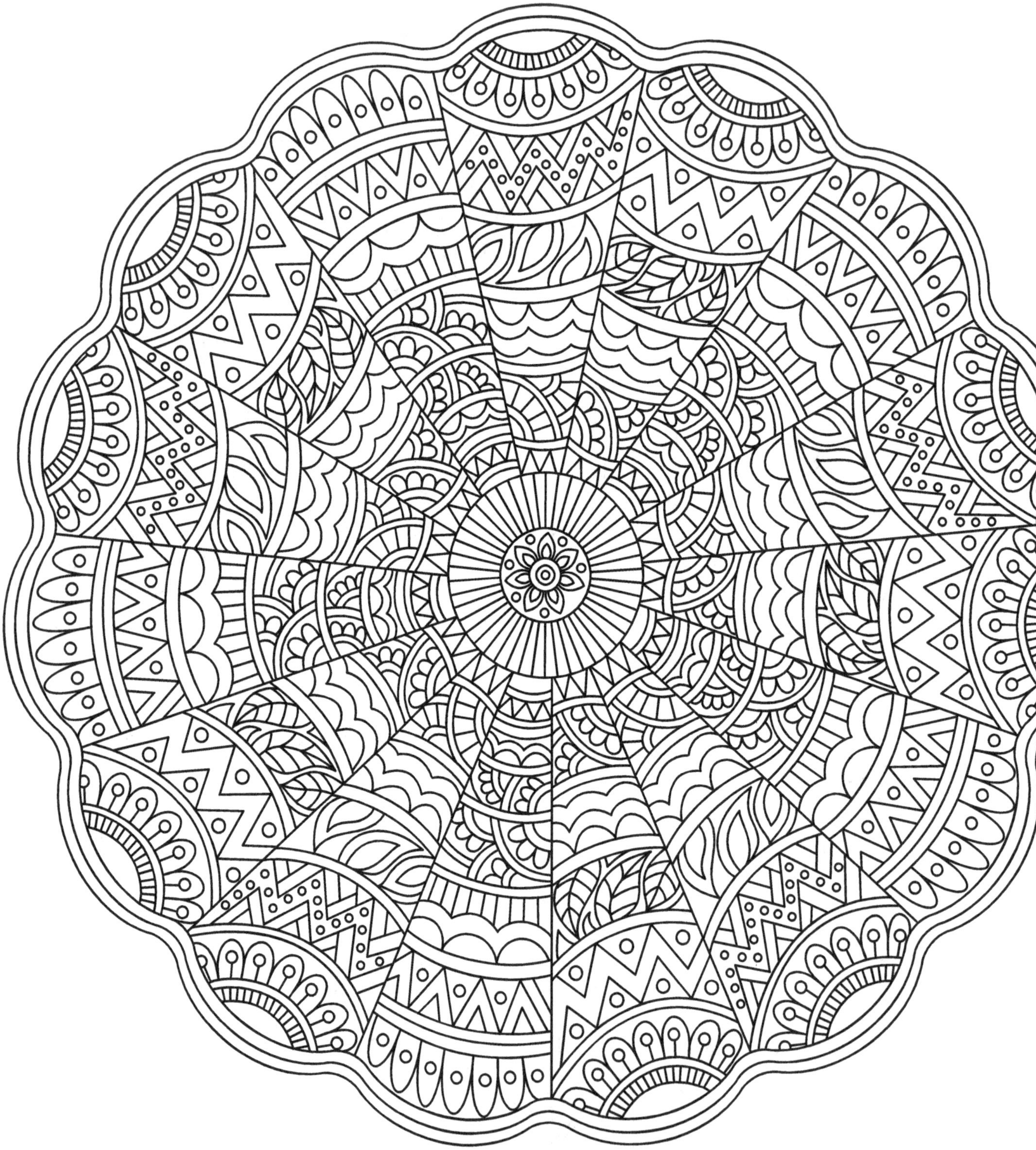

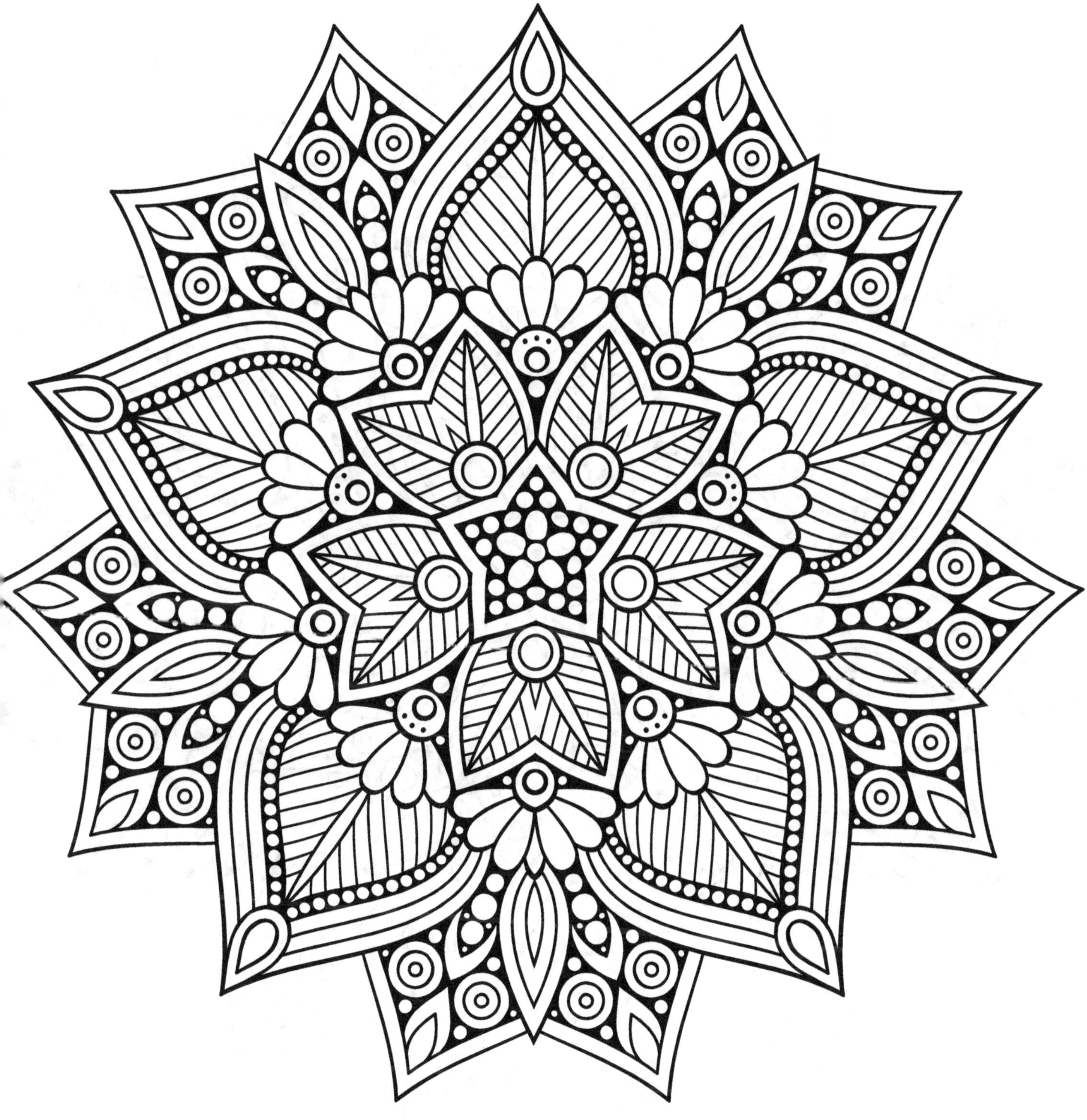

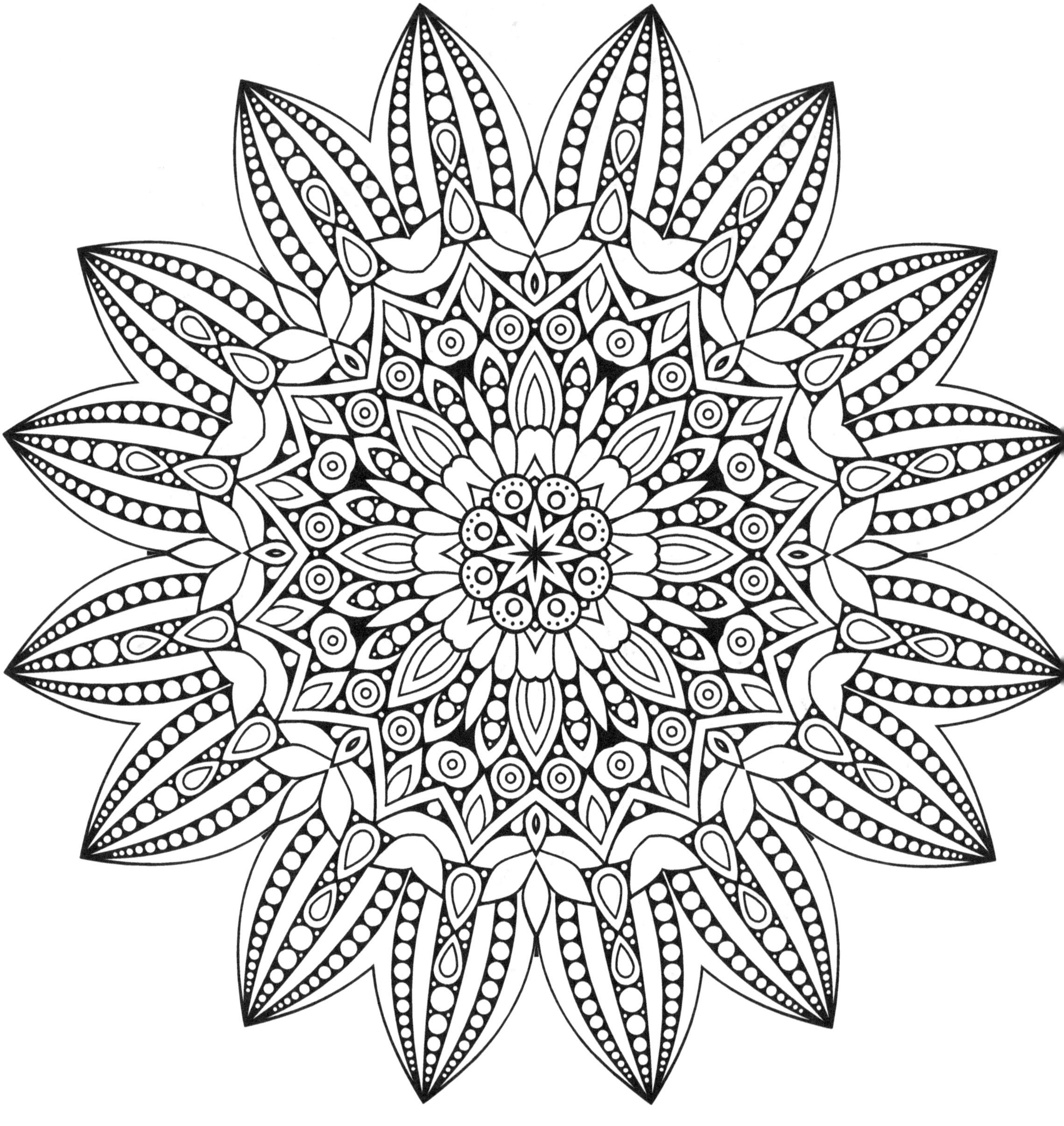

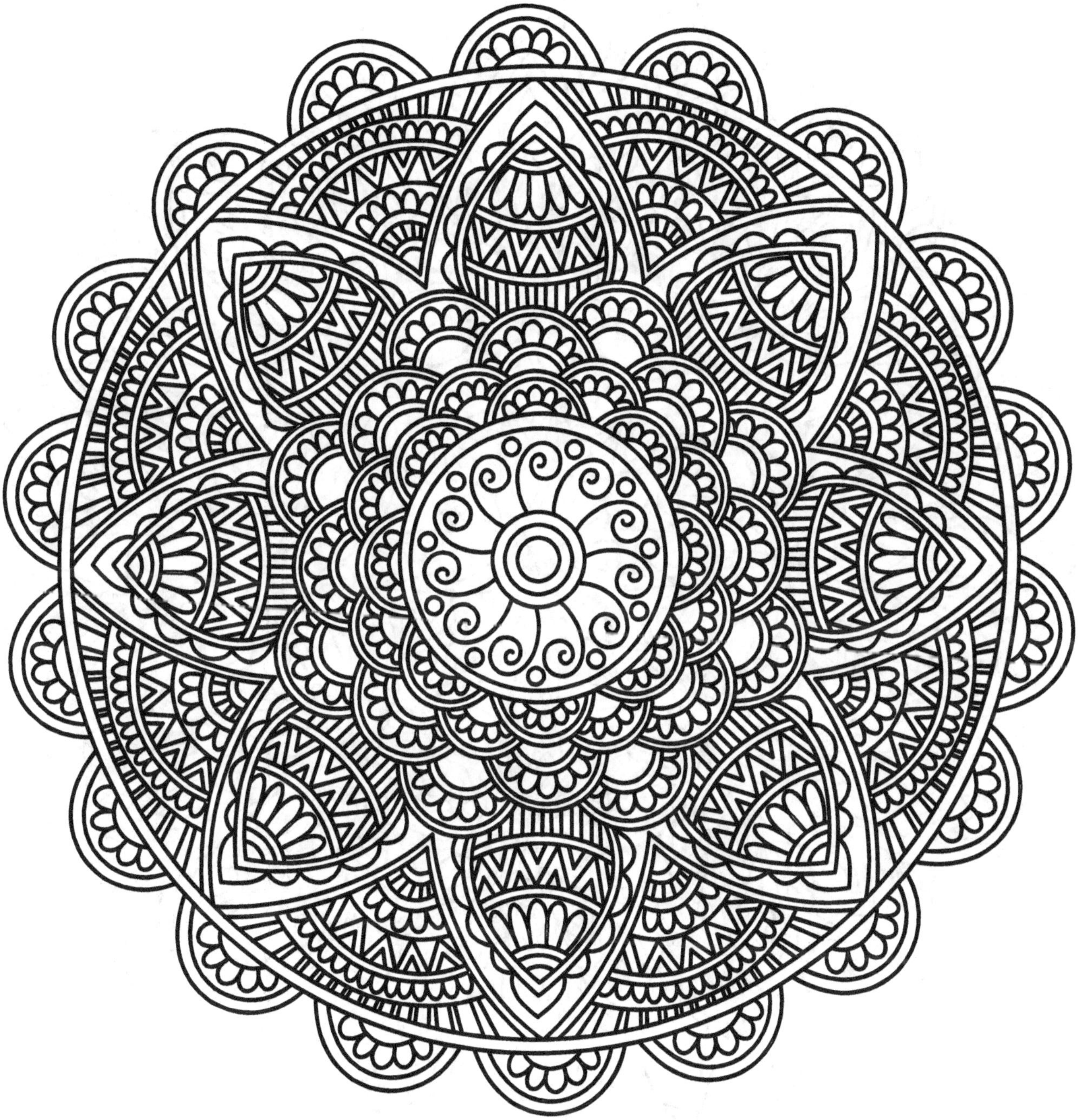

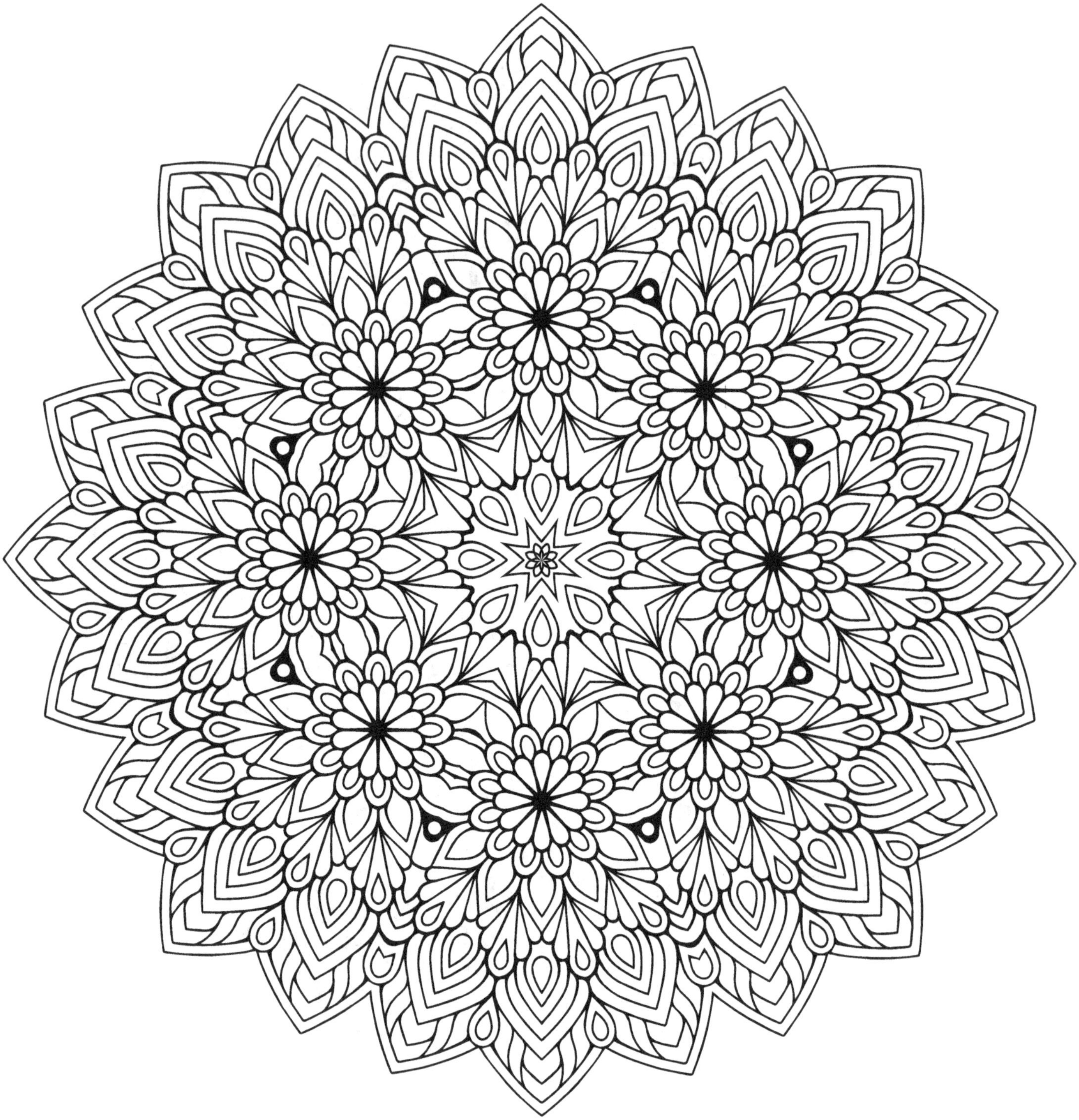

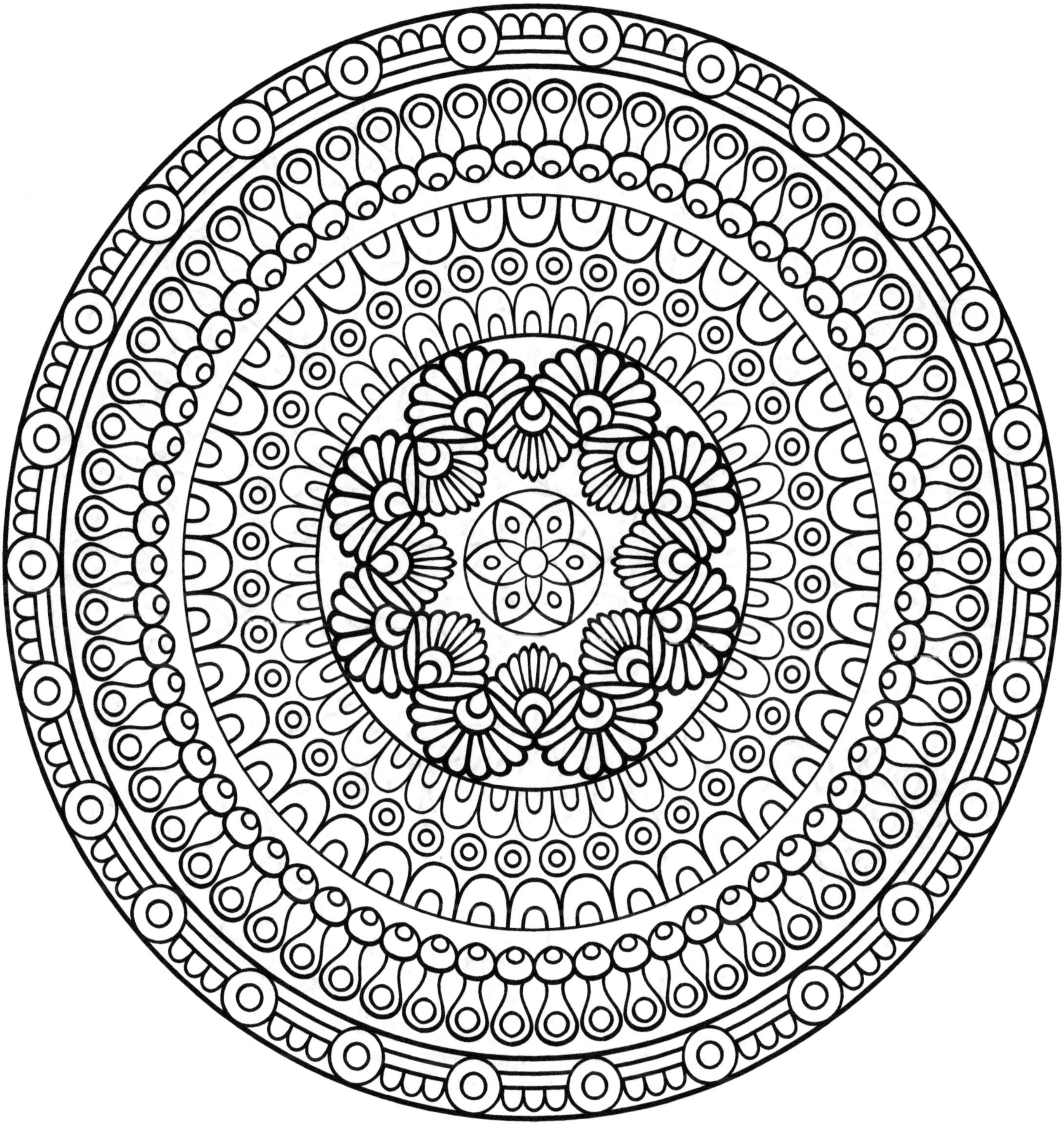

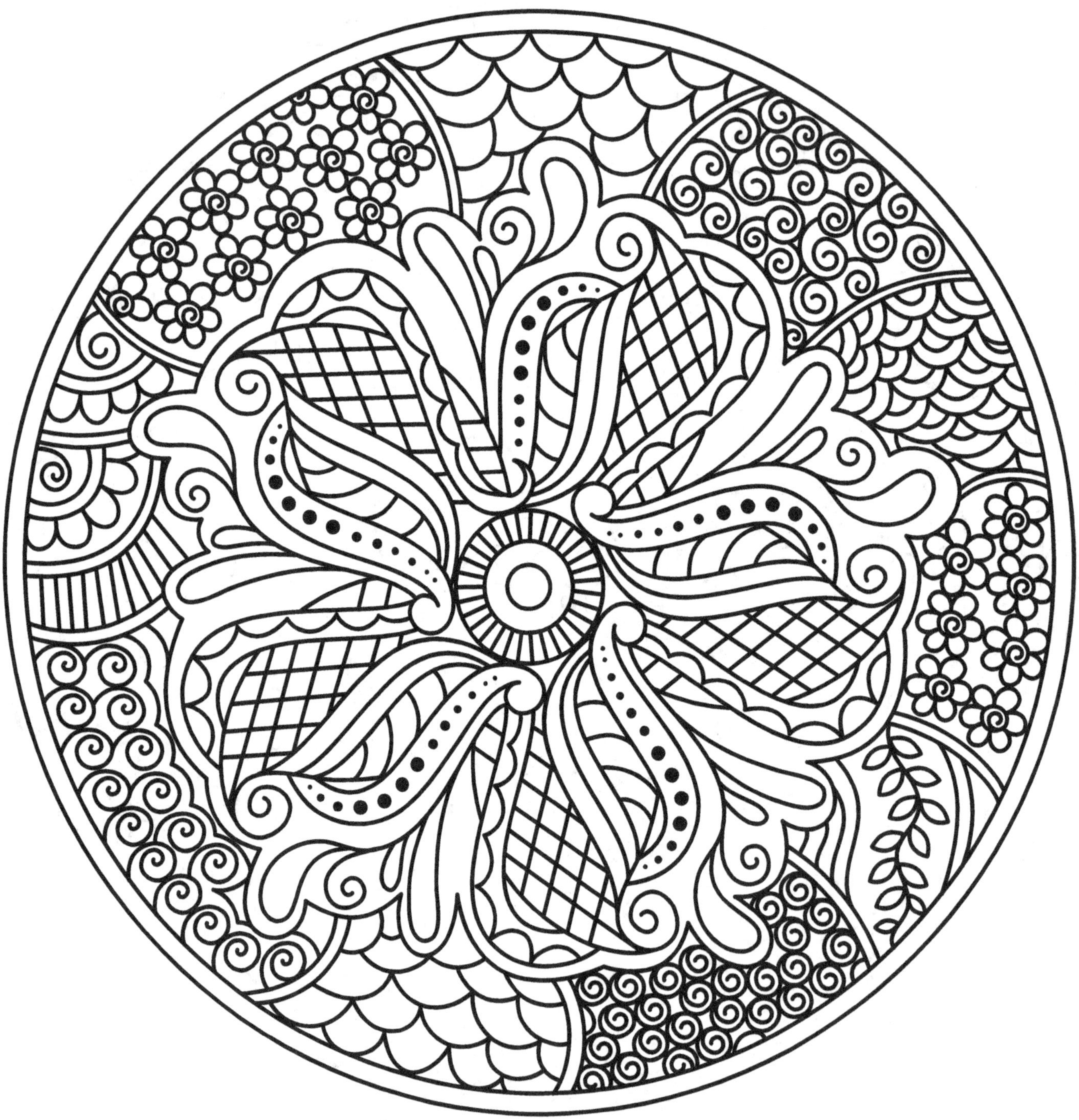

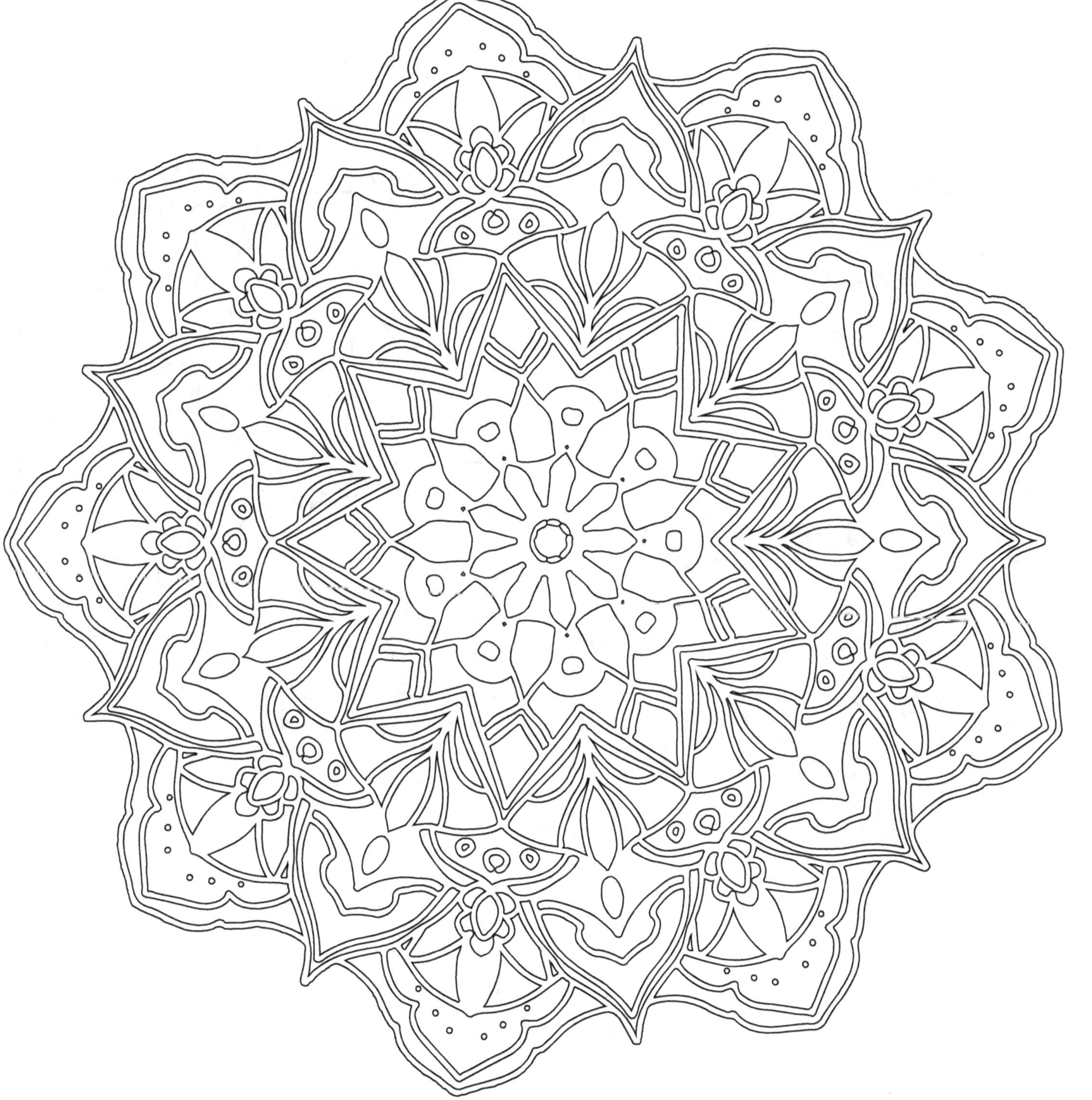

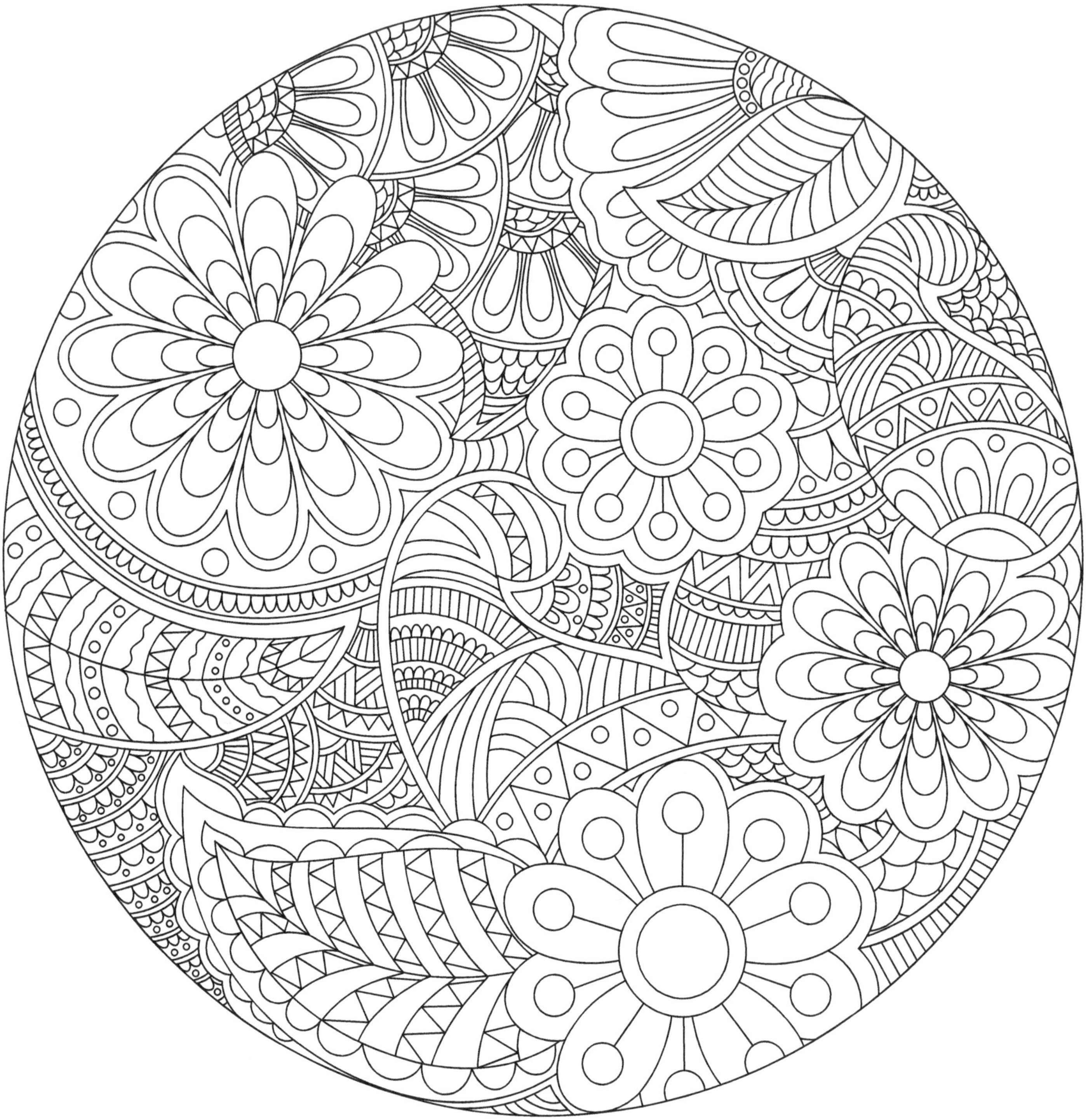

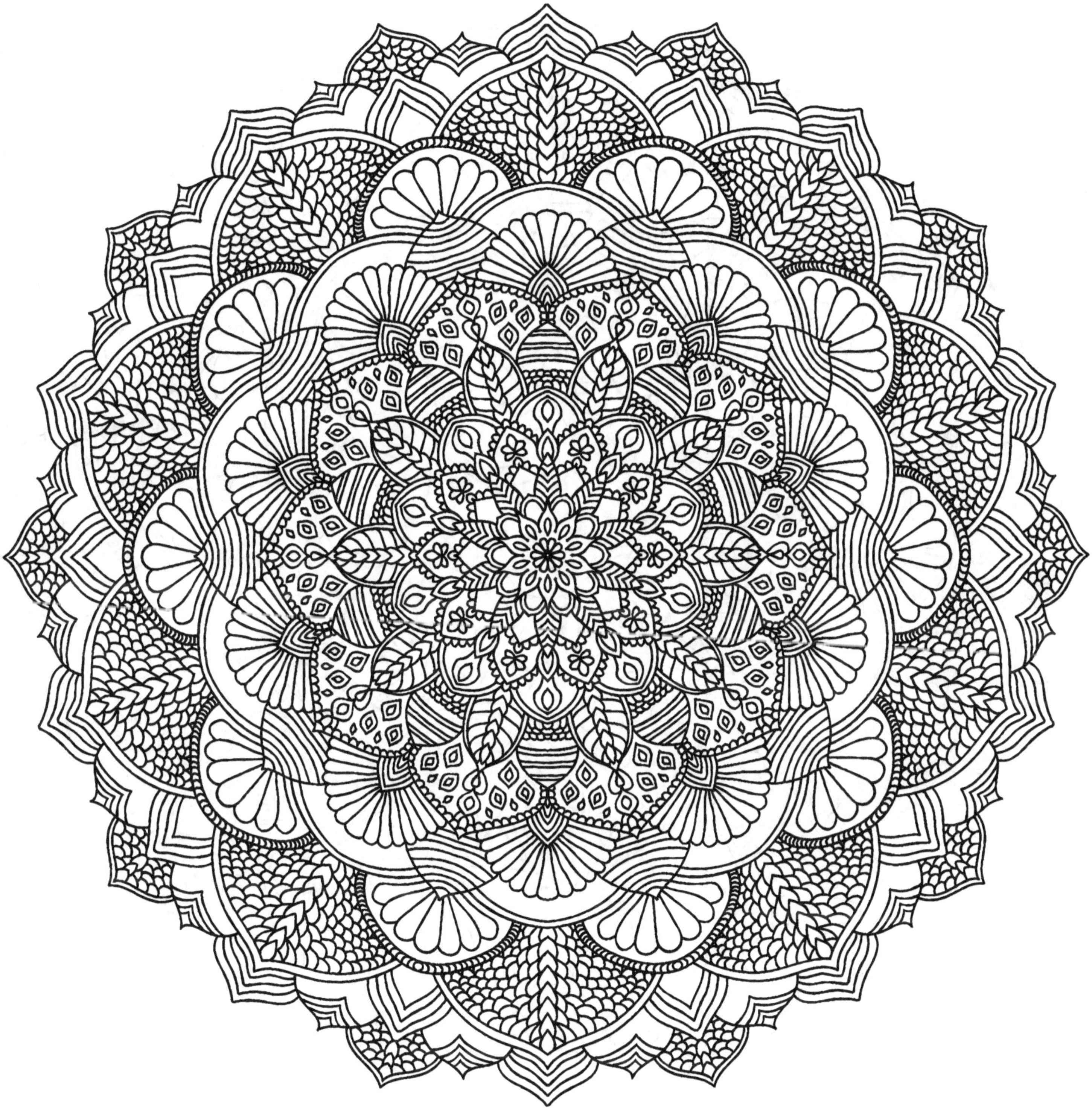

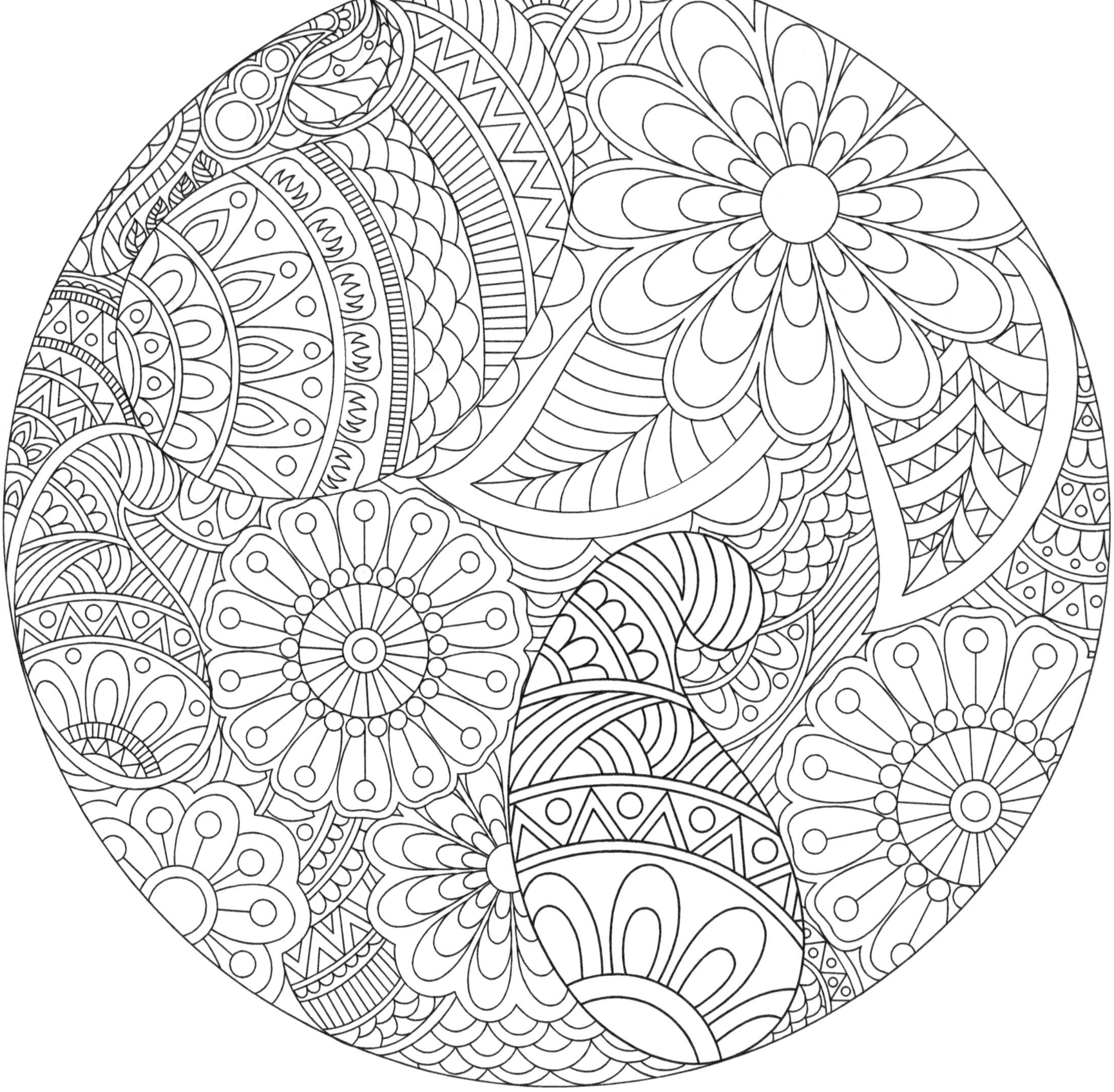

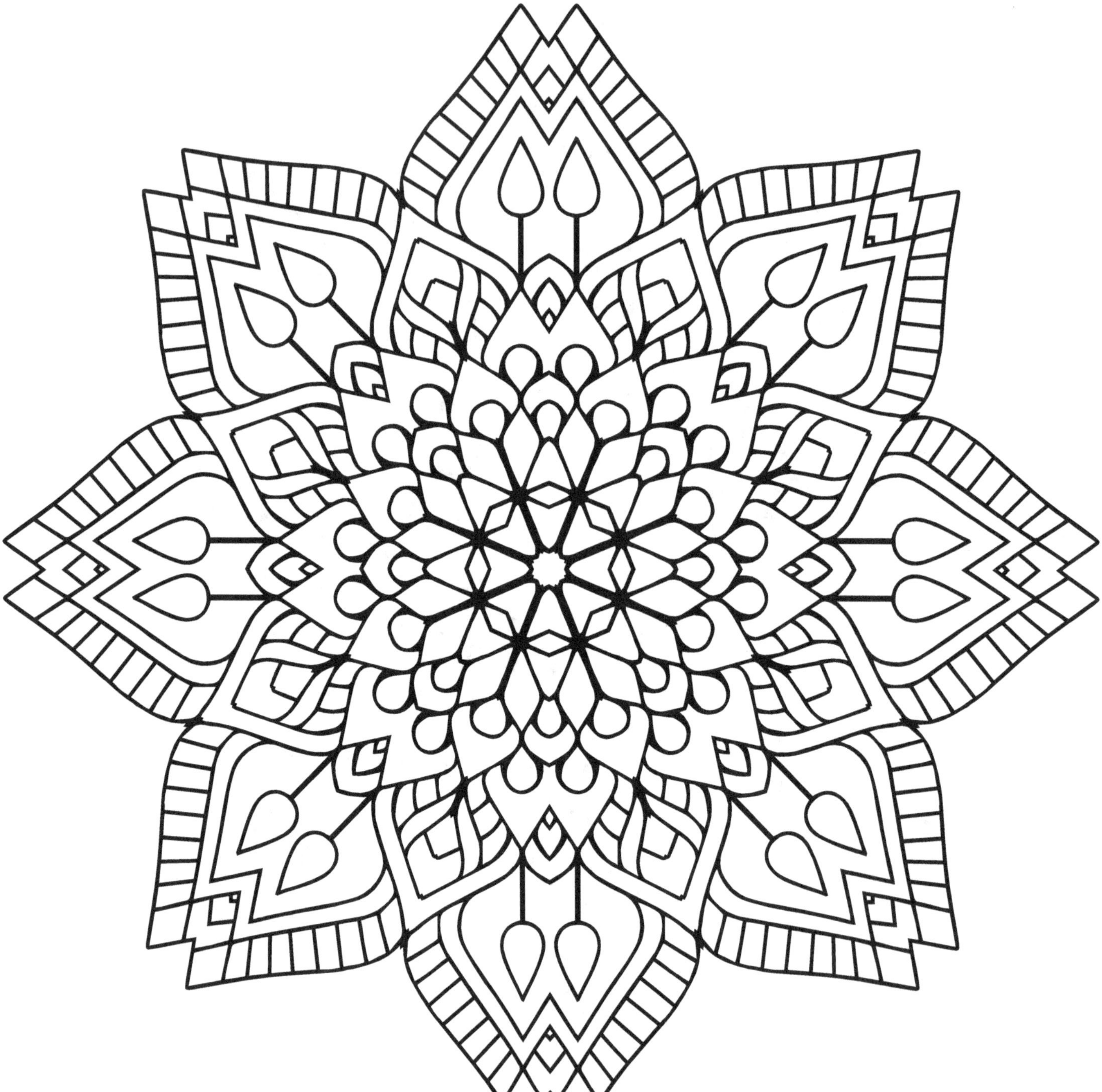

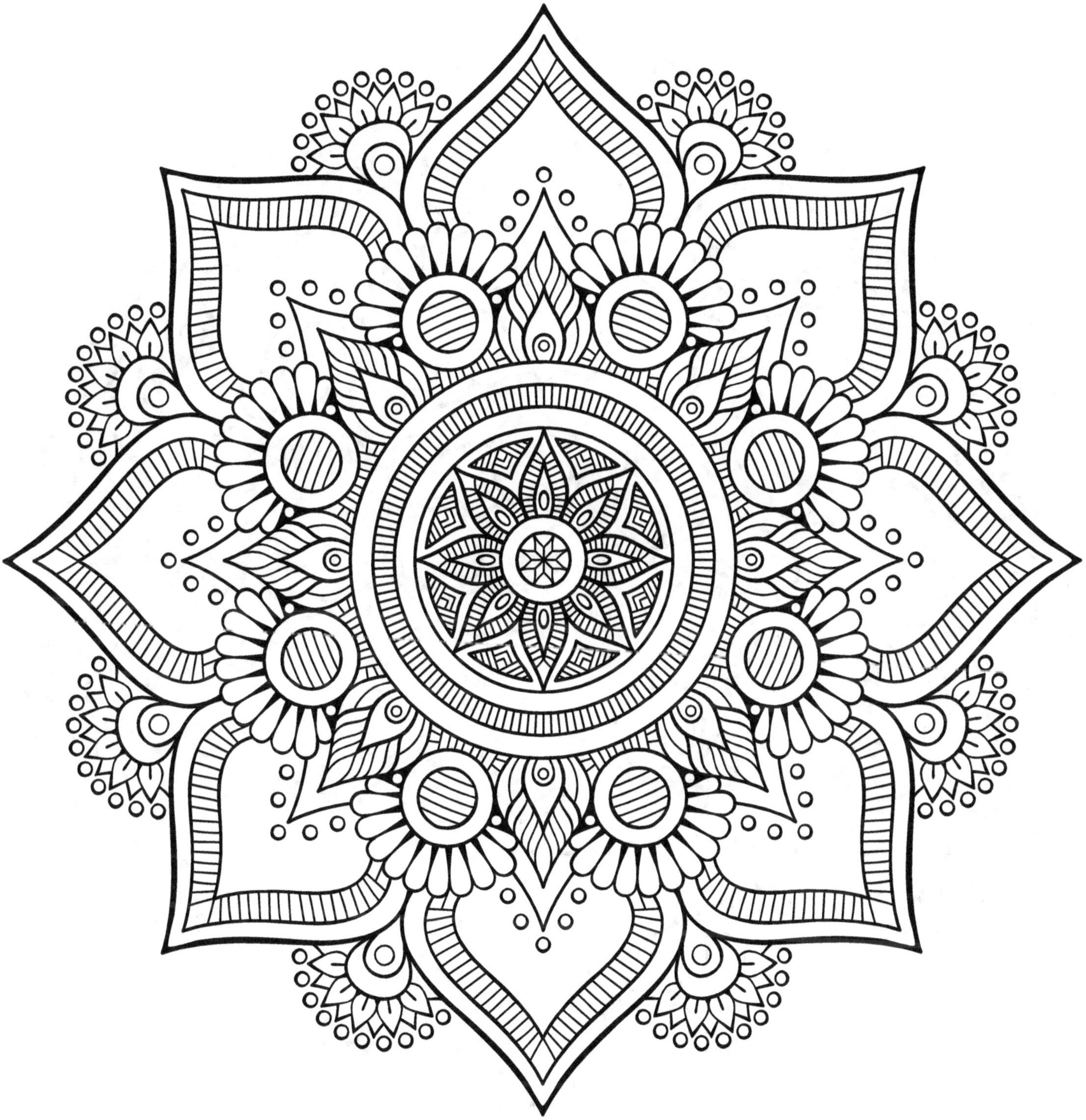

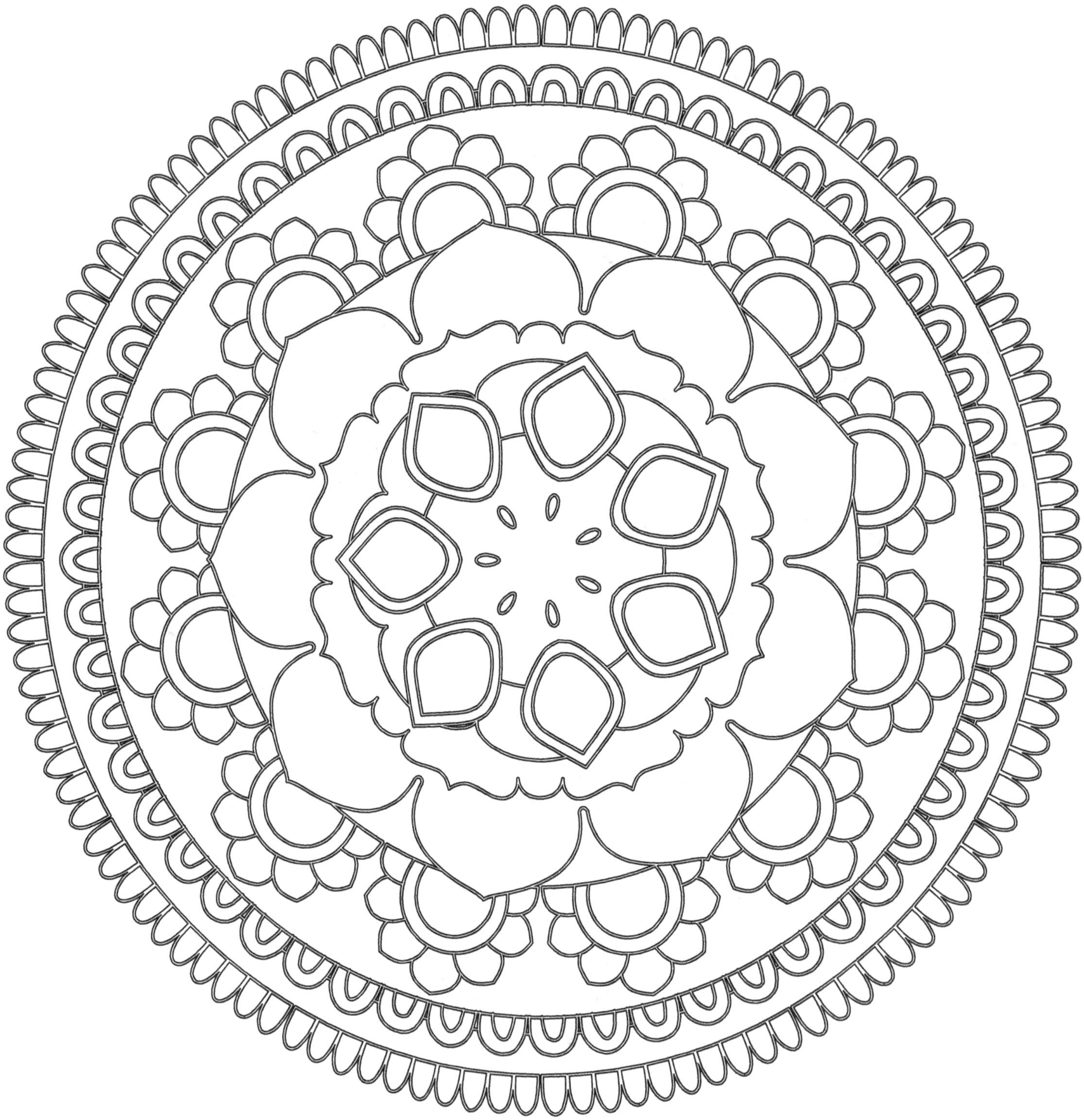

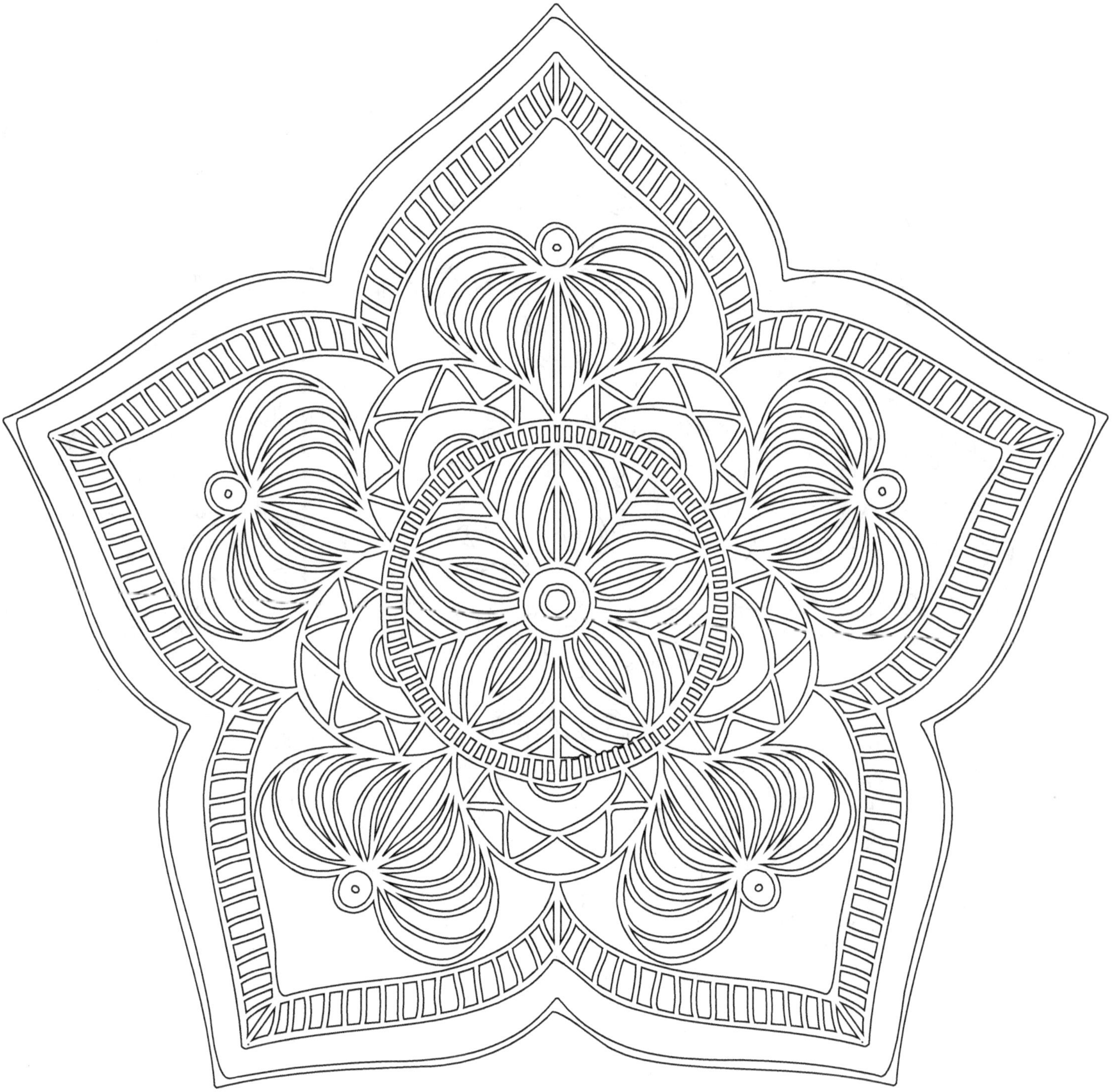

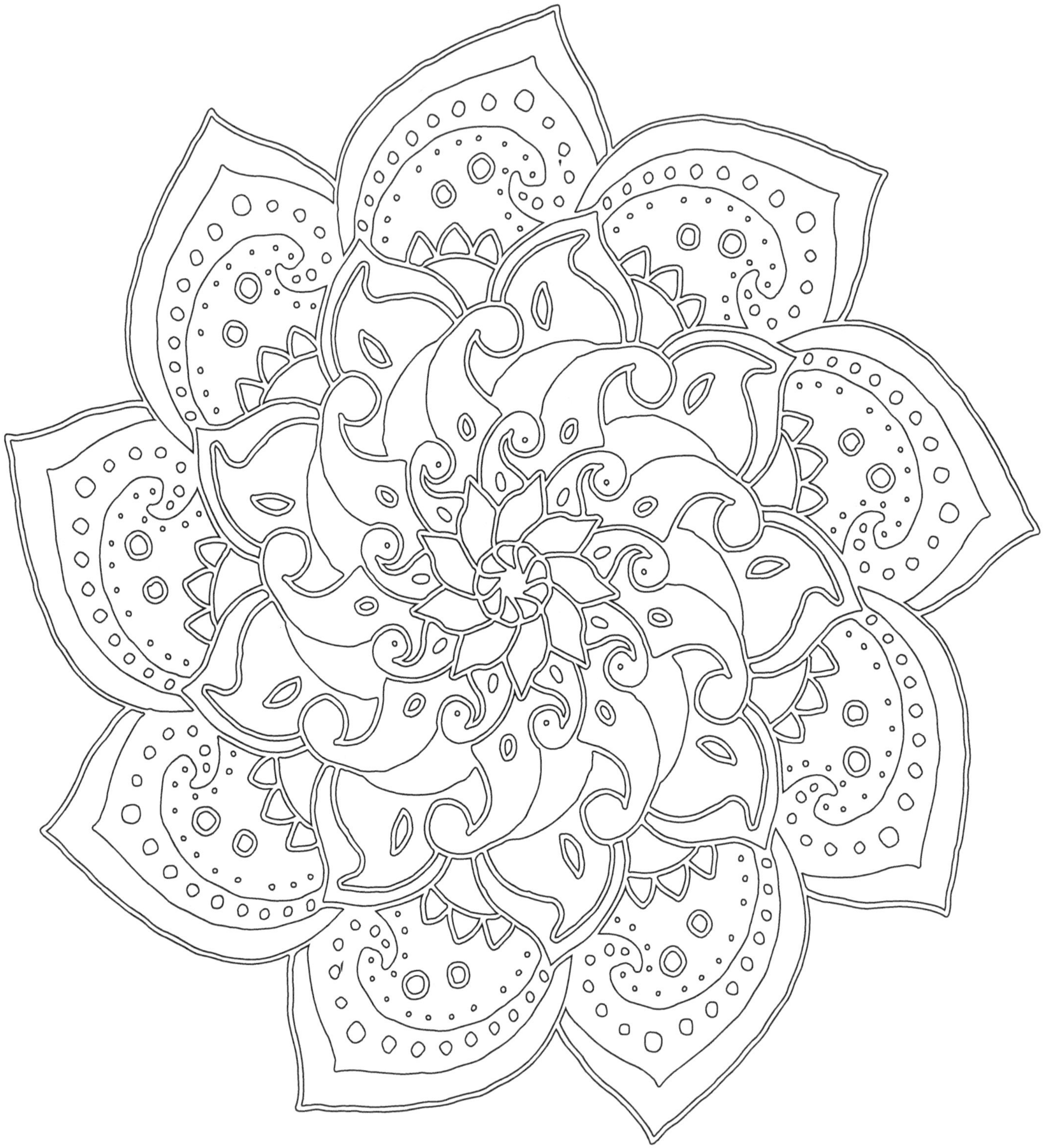

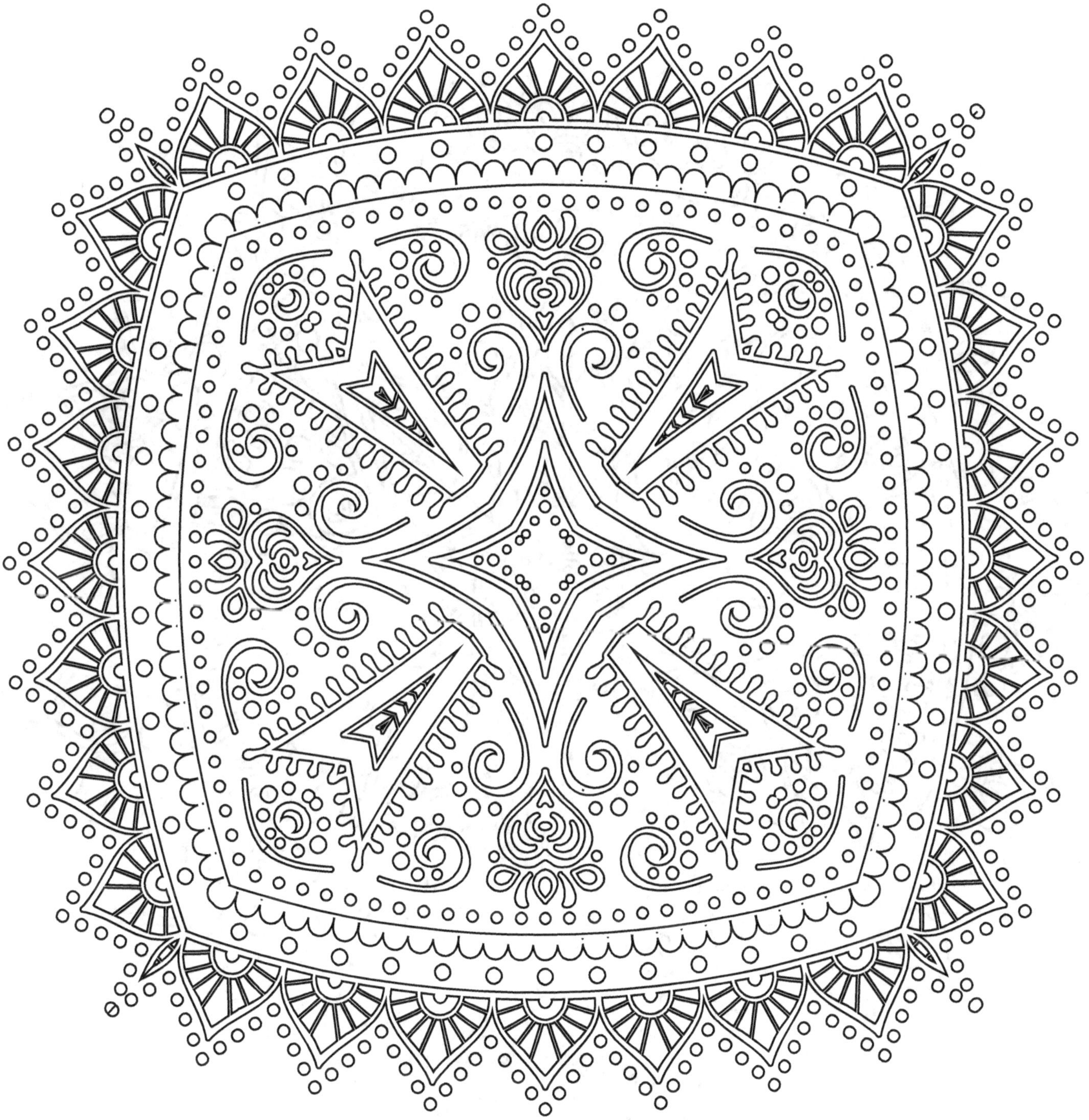

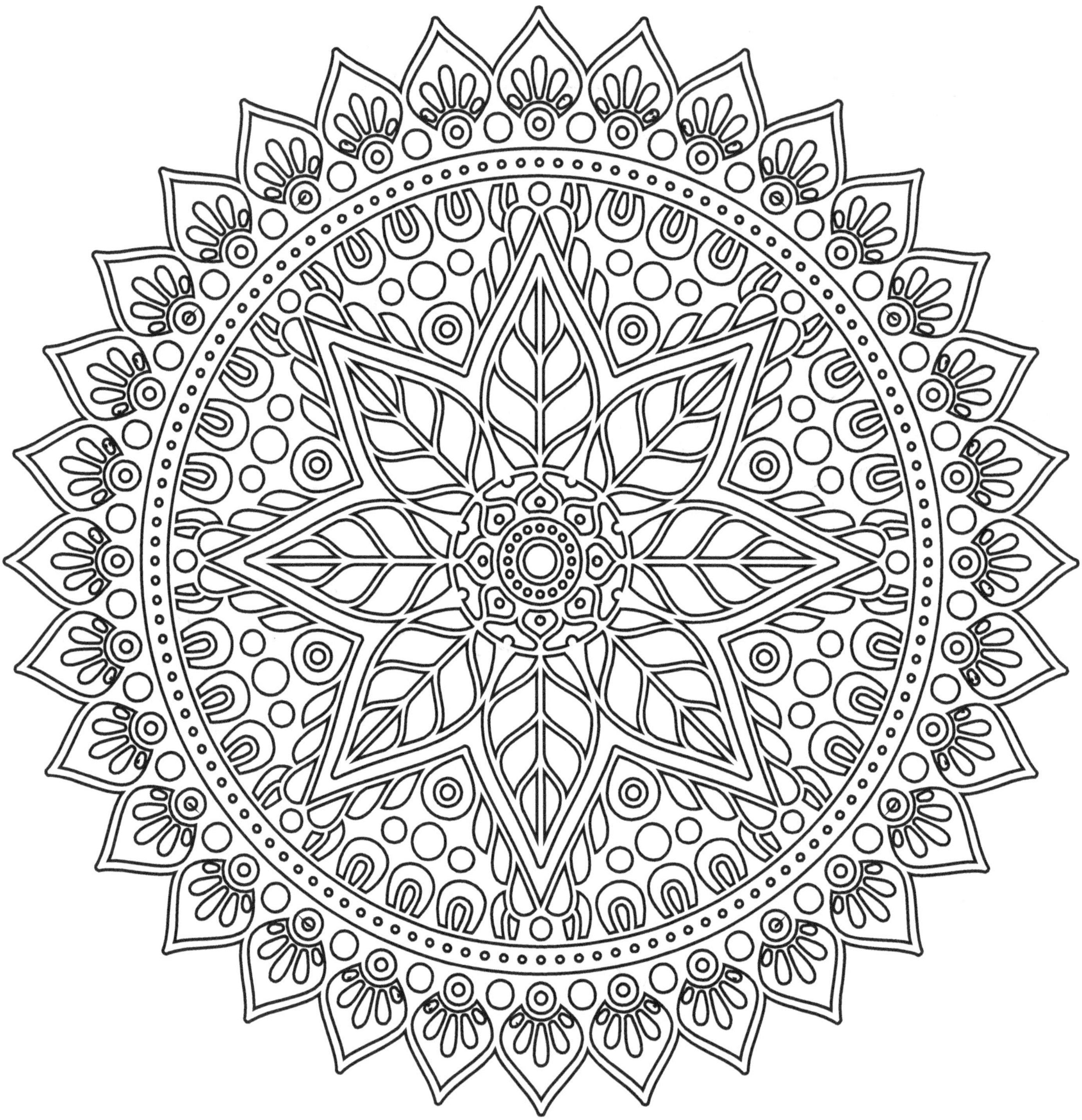

www.ingramcontent.com/pod-product-compliance
Lightning Source LLC
Chambersburg PA
CBHW081535220526
45467CB00010B/3205
* 9 7 9 8 7 1 7 4 6 5 0 7 6 *